AL-IBĀNAH

THE CONCISE CLARIFICATION

VOLUME ONE

BY THE IMĀM

Ibn Battah Al-ʿUkbarī

TRANSLATED BY

Abū Hakeem Bilāl Ibn Ahmad Davis

AL-IBĀNAH AS-SUGHRĀ
The Concise Clarification

by Imām Ibn Battah Al-'Ukbarī
— رَحِمَهُ ٱللَّه —

Volume

1

The Ahādīth and Narrations that Indicate the Compulsory Nature of Clinging to the Sunnah, loving the Sahābah and the Dispraise of Innovation and Splitting in the Religion

TRANSLATION AND COMMENTARY:

Abū Hakeem Bilāl Davis

© COPYRIGHT SALAFI PUBLICATIONS 2021

All rights reserved. No part of this book may be reproduced or reproduced or utilised in any form or by any electronic, mechanical or other means, now known or hereafter invented, including photocopying and recording, without prior permission from the publishers.

FIRST EDITION — AUGUST 2021 CE • DHUL-HIJJAH 1442 AH

Published by Salafi Publications
Twitter — @SalafiPubs
Website — SalafiPublications.com

Distributed by the Salafi Bookstore and Islamic Centre
472 Coventry Road, Small Heath, Birmingham, UK, B10 0UG
Email Address — info@salafibookstore.com
Phone Number — (+44) 0121 773 0033
Twitter — @SalafiBookstore

Design and typeset done in-house at Salafi Publications
Printed by Mega Print in Turkey

Donate at SalafiBookstore.com/donate

ISBN: 978-1-902727-68-4

Salafi
PUBLICATIONS

Transliteration Table

Consonants

ء ʿ ★	د d	ض dh	ك k
ب b	ذ dh	ط t	ل l
ت t	ر r	ظ dh	م m
ث th	ز z	ع ʿ	ن n
ج j	س s	غ gh	ھـ h
ح h	ش sh	ف f	و w
خ kh	ص s	ق q	ي y

★ — The *hamza* may be denoted as an apostrophe, and it may also be denoted by way of an open vowel at the start of a word.

Vowels

SHORT	ـَ a	ـِ i	ـُ u
LONG	ـَا ā	ـِي ī	ـُو ū
DIPHTHONGS	ـَو aw	ـَي ay

Contents

Translator's Introduction

بِسْـــــمِ اللّهِ الرَّحْمَنِ الرَّحِيـــمِ

Indeed, all praise is due to Allāh, we praise him, we seek his aid and we seek his forgiveness. We see refuge in Allāh from the evils within ourselves and from the evil outcomes of our actions. Whomsoever Allāh guides there is none to misguide and whomever Allāh misguides there is none to guide aright. I bear witness that Allāh alone is worthy of worship and I bear witness that Muhammad is His slave and Messenger.

Allāh Almighty said,

> "O you who believe, fear Allāh as He should be feared and do not die except as Muslims" — SŪRAH ĀLI-IMRĀN (3): 102

And He said:

> "O mankind, be dutiful to your lord, who created you from a single soul (Adam), and created from him, his wife (Hawwā (Eve)), and from both of them, He brought forth many men and women. And fear Allāh through whom you you ask one another, and (do not cut the relations of) the wombs (kinship). Verily, Allāh is ever an All-Watcher over you." — SŪRAH AN-NISĀ (4): 1

And Allāh Almighty said,

> "O you who believe, fear Allāh and speak upright words. He will correct your deeds and forgive you your sins. And whoever obeys Allāh and His Messenger has won a tremendous victory." — SŪRAH AL-AHZĀB (33): 70-71

Verily, the most truthful speech is the Book of Allāh, the best guidance is the guidance of Muhammad (ﷺ), and the worst of affairs are newly invented matters. Every newly invented matter is a religious innovation, and every religious innovation is misguidance, and every misguidance is in the Hellfire.

To proceed:

This then, is the first volume of an English translation of one of the monumental authorships of a great and noble Imām of the past; Ibn Battah Al-'Ukbari (رحمه الله). His work, *Ash-Sharhu wal Ibānah 'alā Usulis-Sunnati wad-Diyānah* (الـشَّرْحُ والإِبَانَـة عَـلَى أُصُـول السُّـنَّةِ والدّيَانَـة) (*The Explanation and Clarification of the Fundamentals of the Sunnah and the Religion*) is also known as *Al-Ibānah As-Sughrā* (*The Concise Clarification),* in order to make it distinct from his other, larger compendium, *Al-Ibānah Al-Kubrā (The Major Clarification).* The Imām compiled the treatise, due to the fact that he observed the people becoming distant from the true Sunnah and he saw the widespread nature of innovation in the religion. Coupled with this, he witnessed people clinging to misguided, ignorant individuals, taking them as Imāms and leaders in the religion. Thus, he took to authoring this book, with the noble intent of clarifying that which the Salaf (pious predecessors) of this Ummah were upon of methodology and creed, and the later scholars who followed their path, and of clinging to the Sunnah and refraining from innovations and its people. If it was relevant in his era (The early part of the 4th century after hijra), it is all the more relevant in this time. Thus, we present this English rendition of this most important work, in the hopes that the Ummah takes benefit from it.

We ask Allāh to make this work sincerely for his face and that he benefits the worshippers and the lands by way of it.

We ask Allāh to keep us firm upon this creed until we meet him.

ABŪ HAKĪM BILAL IBN AHMAD DAVIS

Biography of Ibn Battah

His Name:

His name is 'Ubaidillāh Ibn Muhammad Ibn Muhammad Ibn Hamdān Ibn 'Umar Ibn 'Īsā Ibn Ibrāhīm Ibn 'Utbah Ibn Farqad. His lineage ends at the noble companion of the Messenger of Allāh 'Utbah Ibn Farqad (رَضِيَٱللَّهُعَنْهُ).

His Kunyah:

His Kunyah is Abū 'Abdillāh Al-'Ukbari and his title is Ibn Battah, it is said that *Battah* was a title given to one of his forefathers.

His Birth:

He was born in the year 304H.

His Upbringing and Study:

Ibn Battah was born into a household of knowledge and Sunnah. His father was a man of knowledge and Hadīth. His father had a special concern for him and taught him Hadīth from a young age. He then permitted him to travel to Baghdād before he reached the age of ten.

'Alī Ibn Ahmad Ibn Busr said: "Abū 'Abdillāh Ibn Battah said to me: 'My father had business partners in Baghdād. From them was an individual called Abū Bakr. So he said to my father: *"Send your son with me to study Hadīth in Baghdād."* My Father said: *"My son is young!"* So he responded: *"I will carry him with me (i.e. and take care of him)."*

So he carried me with him to Baghdād. I went to Ibn Manī' and someone was reciting Hadīth to him. So someone said: *"Ask the*

Shaikh to bring out his Muʿjam (one of his books)." So I asked his son or his daughters son who said: "He wants Dirhams (i.e. for the reading) so I gave to him and we read his book *Al-Muʿjam* to him, in a private sitting over the period of more or less ten days. That was in 15H or 16H (i.e. 315H or 316H)."

His journeying for knowledge continued until he matured. He travelled to Makka, various military outposts, likewise to Basra and other countries.

When he returned from his travels, he went into isolation and remained in his home for forty years. He was never seen in the marketplaces and rarely seen in public. Although that was the case, he was well known for commanding the good and forbidding the evil when he did leave his home.

His Teachers

From the most well-known and distinguished of his Shuyūkh and teachers:

- Abū Bakr Ahmad Al-Qatiʿi (368H)

- Al-Hasan ibn ʿAlī Al-Barbahārī (329H)

- Abul-Fadl Jaʿfar Al-Qāfilāni (325H)

- Abū Bakr Ahmad Ibn Sulaimān An-Najād (334H)

- Abū Bakr Al-Ismāʿili An-Naisābūrī (324H)

- Abul-Qāsim Al-Baghawī (317H)

- Abū Bakr Al-Bāghandī (312H)

- Abū Bakr Al-Ājjurī (360H)

- Ibn Sāʿīd (318H)

- Ibn Makhlad (331H)

- Abū Bakr ʿAbdul-ʿAzīz Al-Khallāl (363H)

His Students

From the most prominent of his students:

- Ibn Shihāb Al-ʿUkbarī (428H)

- Abū Hafs Al-ʿUkbarī (387H)

- Abū Bakr Az-Zāhid who is known as Ar-Rūshinānī (441H)

- Abū Is-hāq Al-Barmakī (361H)

- Ahmad Ibn ʿAbdillāh Ibn Al-Khadir — well known as As-Sūsanjardī

- Abū ʿAbdillāh Ibn Hāmid Al-Baghdādī

His Works

Imām As Sanʿānī mentioned concerning him: "He was from the Jurists of the Hanbalī School, who authored beneficial works."

Imām Ibn Kathīr mentioned: "He had a huge and extensive number of works, in various sciences."

It is said that his works number more than 100 authorships, from those works:

- Al-Ibānatul-Kubrā

- Al-Ibānatus-Sughrā

- As-Sunan

- Al-Manāsik (Concerning the Rites of Hajj)

- Al-Imāmu Dhāmin

- Al-Inkār ʿalā Man Qasara bi Kutubis Suhufil-Ūlā

- Al-Inkār ʿalā Man Akhadhal Qurʾān Minal Mus-haf

- An-Nahi ʿan Salātin Nāfilati baʿdal ʿAsri wa baʿdal Fajr

- Tahrīm An-Namīmah

- Salātul-Jamā'ah

- Man'ul Khurūj ba'd Al-Adhāni wal-Iqāmah li Ghairil-Hājah

- Ahkām An-Nisā'

- Al-'Uzlah

- Ibtāl Al-Hiyal

- Tahrīm An-Nabīdh

To name but a few.

His Creed:

The Imām was known for being a scholar of the Sunnah and correct 'Aqīdah. He was a well-known follower of the pious predecessors and their narrations. This is apparent from his writings and authorships.

Imām Adh-Dhahabī said concerning him:

| "He was an Imām in the Sunnah"

Statements of the scholars concerning him:

Al-'Atīqi said: "He was righteous — a shaikh whose supplications were responded to!"

Ibn Kathīr said: "He was one of the 'Ulamā of the Hanbalīs"

Adh-Dhahabī mentioned: "Ibn Battah, the Imām, the example, the staunch worshipper, the Jurist, the Scholar of Hadīth, the Shaikh of 'Irāq."

He also said: "Ibn Battah was from the major Imāms, a person of asceticism, and jurisprudence, and Sunnah and Ittibā' (Following of the Salaf)."

Abul Fat-h Al-Qawās said: "I mentioned to Abū Saʿīd Al-Ismāʿīlī Ibn Battah and his knowledge and his asceticism. So he went to meet him. When he returned, he said: *'He has surpassed the description!'*"

His Station in Hadīth

While Ibn Battah had the station that he had among the scholars of Hadīth of the past, and though he was revered by his teachers and his students, it should be mentioned, that there occurred some criticism for Ibn Battah from some of the scholars of Hadīth. From those who criticised him, was Imām Khatīb Al-Baghdādi. His criticism of Ibn Battah was from the angle of his memory. A number of the people of knowledge came to the defence of Imām Ibn Battah, from them Ibnul-Jawzī in his book of history *Al-Muntadham*. He also authored a separate work defending Ibn Battah entitled: *Al-Intisār li bin Battah* (*The Defence of Ibn Battah*). Similarly, from those who have defended Imām Ibn Battah, the great Yemeni scholar of Hadīth of this era, the one who has been referred to as the Imām Dhahabī of this time, Shaikh ʿAbdur-Rahmān Ibn ʿAlī Al-Muʿallimī in his book *At Tankīl* (1/340-348). The balanced position concerning him though is that while no one will dispute that he is an Imām described with piety, asceticism, upright religion, and vast knowledge, there is no doubt, however, that the reputable scholars of criticism, have concluded that he had an issue in terms of his memory.

Al-Hāfidh Adh-Dhahabī mentions concerning him: "He is truthful and trustworthy, though they (i.e. the scholars of Hadīth) spoke concerning his precision."

Al-Hāfidh Ibn Hajr likewise said: "He is an Imām, though he did have some errors (i.e. in the precision of his narrations)."

This balanced position becomes clear as we examine the text of the book that we have before us. We will see, that on occasions, his version of some Hadīth and narrations do not exist in the popular sources of Hadīth. In fact, we see in the works of some of the scholars of the Hadīth, that he may have narrated a particular narration by way of, that they collect the narration with slightly variant wording to the version collected by the Imām himself. This is one of the means used to detect whether or not a particular scholar of hadith, is as precise as the well-known mountains of knowledge, by seeing how often he agrees with or opposes, the narrations of the well-known precise narrators. These variations are detected in some of the narrations collected by Imām Ibn Battah, though the origin of the narration may generally be correct and present in other works, but with slightly variant wording. These occasional errors do not slight the monumental nature of this work.

His Death:

He passed away in the year 387H and was 83 years old at the time of his death.

Sources:

- *Al-'Ibar* of Adh-Dhahabī (3/35)

- *Tabaqātul Hanābilah* of Ibn Abī Ya'lā (3/256)

- *Al-Bidāyatu Wan Nihayah* of Ibn Kathīr (11/343)

- *Al-Ansāb* of As-Sam'āni (3/243)

- *Lisānul Mizān* of Al-Hāfidh Ibn Hajr (3/133)

- *Siyar A'lāmin Nubalā'* of Adh-Dhahabī (16/529)

About his book: *Al-Ibānah As-Sughrā - The Concise Clarification of the Creed*

The Imām Ibnu Battah authored his book *Al-Ibānah As-Sughrā*, due to what he had observed in his era from people abandoning the Sunnah and embarking upon the path of innovations in belief and practice, he decided to write a concise work that would highlight the true sunnah and the path that the pious predecessors of this Ummah were upon, in creed and methodology and action. He collected within it, verses from the book of Allāh, statements from the prophet, narrations from the companions and their successors and the consensus of the earliest of generations in issues of belief and action. This work bears witness (through narrations of the pious predecessors) to that which was mentioned by one of the main teachers of the author, Imāmul-Barbahārī in his concise authorship *Sharhus-Sunnah*. This work of his teacher, summarises well, the plethora of statements that have come from the salaf concerning creed.

Since there is a group striving hard to claim that the work of Imām Al-Barbahārī is not correctly attributed to him, the reader will see clearly in this book authored by perhaps his foremost student, that these statements were not some strange fringe opinions falsely attributed to an Imām, but that these were, in truth, the positions held by the best of generations. The work, therefore, comprises the creed, methodology and belief of the pious predecessors and examples of their statements and attitudes towards a number of deviant methodologies with a view to returning the Ummah back to that which the earliest generations were upon, those who the messenger described as the best of generations.

Upon the authority of 'Abdullāh Ibn Mas'ūd who said that the Prophet (صَلَّى اللهُ عَلَيْهِ وَسَلَّمَ) said: "The best of the people is my generation, then those who follow them, then those who follow them."

Shaikh Muhammad Ibn Sālih Al-'Uthaimīn mentioned concerning this hadīth:

> "His statement *'The best of people'* is evidence that his generation was the best [absolutely]. Therefore, his companions were better than the *'Hawāriyyūn'* (the Disciples of Jesus) and they are better than the seventy chosen leaders selected by Musā [from the Children of Isrā'il].
>
> This superiority is general and refers to their class broadly, and not as it relates to specific individuals. That is not to say: that this means, that there does not exist among the Tābi'i Tābi'īn anyone that may have been better than any of the Tābi'īn.

Nor [does it mean] that none of the Tābiʿīn could be more knowledgeable than [some of the] Sahābah. As far as the virtue of the Sahābah then no one can attain that other than a Sahābī, no one can outdo them in that. As for Knowledge and worship, then there may be among some of those who have come after the companions, individuals who may have been better than some of them in knowledge and worship."

Concerning the Era that the Imām lived in and some of the Causes for his Authoring the Book, he mentions:

"Indeed, when I observed what has overcome the people, and what they have made manifest, that which has overcome them and caused them to deem evil desires, false opinion, distortion of the sunnah and substitution of the religion something good. To the extent that it has become a cause for their division, and an opening of the door of trials, blindness of their hearts, splitting of their ranks and destruction of their unity. They have thrown the book behind their backs and have taken the ignorant and the misguided as lords in their affairs, after knowledge has come to them from their lord.

They used (false) argumentation in that which they claim, and used the witness of conjecture as a definitive authority. Falsehood is proof for them in matters of their creed. They have blindly followed in their religion, those who have no knowledge, concerning affairs they have no evidence for in the book (of Allāh), neither do they have upon it, the proof of consensus..."

When he observed this, he embarked upon authoring the book with a view to rectifying affairs.

Sections within the Book

The author categorised the book into four sections:

1. The Aḥādīth and narrations that indicate the compulsory nature of clinging to the Sunnah, loving the Sahābah and the dispraise of innovation and splitting in the religion.

2. A discussion of the creed of Ahlus-Sunnah wal-Jamā'ah. That which the 'Ulamā of the Ummah have consensus upon. The like of which the Muslims should not be ignorant of, and Allāh — Glorified be His name — will not excuse the one who neglects it.

3. A discussion of a number of important affairs, both compulsory and supererogatory, related to the Muslims character and mannerisms, the like of which the Muslim has great need for, encompassing various areas of Jurisprudence. He chooses from these issues, in particular, those affairs that distinguish the people of Sunnah from other than them.

4. A discussion of various types of innovation that the people (of innovation) brought about during his time. Actions that have no basis in the book of Allāh, nor any narration substantiating it from the pious predecessors.

Thus, our translation of this tremendous authorship, will manifest in four volumes, reflecting these four sections of the book. This first volume being *"The Aḥādīth and Narrations that Indicate the Compulsory Nature of Clinging to the Sunnah, loving the Sahābah and the Dispraise of Innovation and Splitting in the Religion"*.

I ask Allāh to make this work beneficial to the Ummah, and that he grants us sincerity in statement and action, and that he accepts this humble effort, and records it in our scroll of good deeds on the day of judgement.

ABŪ HAKĪM BILĀL IBN AHMAD DAVIS

بسم الله الرحمن الرحيم

الحمد لله الذي اسبغ علينا نعمه وظاهر علينا رحمته وحملنا من اجله قدرا واعظمها

والصلاة والسلام على محمد وعلى آله وصحبه

وبعد فان هذا المعرفته والقوة او يزونه ... امر اتباع ...

... الصلاة والسلام على محمد وسن ... ما اصطفى ... الاسلام ... وقال السنه

والمناهل وعلم الامام الذي ... علم وكان فصل امر الله عليه ... وصلى الله عليه المرتضى

ورسوله المصطفى ارسله ... جنته وإياب ... وحد اننه والدعا الله بالحكمه

والموعظه ... والحرص على الشرائع الظاهره والسنن الزاكيه والاخلاق

الفاضله وسلم ... ونسو نوله لله لصواب الامور وصلح الحال ونسله ان

يجعل عز ضاقنا ... من ذلك ... وجهه وانا رضاه ويحبه لقول

... وضعوا او نوا اناله ... موفورا ثم أما بعد فان اي الله ...

... ... به اواب الصواب ونقص ... العصر من هذا الخطا

... انه وبجمع ودود ... المارين به ان المارات ما فرعمر الناس

واطهروه وعلى عليهم فاس ... من فظائع الامور وقد ... المراد ...

سنتهم وترتيل بهم حتى صار ذلك بسالفهم وفي حباب ... والعمل على امورهم

ونشر القهير وتعزيز جماعتهم بسد الكاذب واطهوهم والحذر والجهال

والصلاة ... اموزهم من جهه مظاهر العلوم بهم ... اسمعلو الحمور ...

فيما يدعون وطعوا الشهاد ... عليها بالطوز ... لجوزا البهار فيما يفعلون

وطاوا اسهم البر لا يعلمون ومع برهان لهم به في الغاز ... وبعده عدم ...

من الاجاع به وابر الله لهم ما الغت الساطن على اواه لخراكم المجلس

عز وجل ورَدَ كرةٌ في كتابه من لزوم الجماعة والنهي عن الفُرقة وقال عز وجل
ولاعتصموا بحبل الله جميعاً ولا تفرّقوا ثم بهذا المُوحدون باذوتُ جماعة اللذين
فقال وكانتوا كالذين تفرّقوا واختلفوا بعد ما جاءهم البينات وأولئك لهم
عذابٌ عظيمٌ نامن الله بذلك عز وتعالى بالاجتماع على دينه وطاعته وقال
عز وجل وما أمر الا وللعبدا الله مخلصين له الدين جُنفاً ويقيموا الصلاة ويؤتوا
الزكاة وذلك دين القيمة وقال تعالى أن الله يحب الذين يقاتلوا في سبيله صفاً
كانهم بنيان مرصوصٌ وما أمرنَه للمؤمنين بايه مخالف عنهم ذلك عهدهم
وطمع فيهم من جاشتهم وترك مجالستهم الى سماع له خطاب وتخطيهم
فقال تبارك وتعالى بذلك لقاعدة في الكتاب اذا سمعتم اياتِ الله يكفر
بها ويستهزأ بها فلا بعدوا وأحمدى بحصوا في حديث عنه أخرى اذا اعلم
أن الله جامع المنافقين والكافرين في جهنم جميعاً ثم أمر رسول الله صلى الله
عليه وسلم البر خلواعنه بحبر انفذوا ما بينهم وأمرهان تعز لاوايتاحمتى
أنزل الله عز وجل ورسُوله وقال على الله تعليهم اولئك أهل الفضل على
بنى اسرائيل كان الرجل يلقى الخاه فيقول باهذا أتق الله ودع ما تصنع
فانه لا يحل لك ثم يلقاه من العذ فلا يمنعه ذلك أن يكون أكله وشربه
ته وفعله فلما فعلوا ذلك ضرب الله قلوب بعضهم ببعض قال لعن
الذين كفروا بني اسرائيل على لسان داود وعيسى بن مريم ذلك بما عصوا وكانوا
يعتدون كانوا لا يتناهون عن منكر فعلوه وقال كصلى الله عليه مثل القائم على حدود الله
والداهن بها مثل قوم استسهموا على سفينه في البحر فاصاب بعضهم أسفلها
وبعضهم أعلاها وكان الذين في أسفلها جون ويستمرون الماء ونصون

مراعاة دبيب الضلال وحرزوا المعالى بن محمد بناب البدع أظهر الجميع ربع
تسبه على العقول ومن سلجلى الصد وزنا لايقوم ولعرضها بشر وكانت
تظليمها قدم الأمر عن الله بالعلم وايده بالبينة وكلم جمع في هذا الكتاب
طرفا ما اسمعناه وحلاما ما نقلناه عن آمد الدين وأعلام المسلمين بما قالوه
لاغر ورسول الله صلى الله عليهم رب العالمين وبما حض عليه مراعته
من المرسين وما أعربوا من المسك لسنته وسلوك طريقته والاقتداء هديه
والاقتفا لاثره ودين من بعد ذلك للجرائم السنة ثم الحوض في الرد وما
امر الله عز وجل به ورسوله لدى وصى الله عليهم من لزوم الجماعه ومبانه اهل الربع
والعزو والشناجه وماليوم وما لوا من أهل السر من الجاهنه والمبانه من خالف عليهم علي الربع
عهرهم وولج في دينهم ونصر لبهم وجماعهم فمن اثر ذلك شرج السنه
من اجماع الامه وأفارق لامته ونطارق اهل لله فجمعين ذلك مع السبع
المسلمين جمله وكاهدر الله تبارك اسمه من اصاعه وأبسط الدين خالفه
وطعن عليه من دخصعته لما استهل الامر وذلك قدمه لانبيا لله المبين
وعموعن بشره وجبن خالف سنه المصطفى والراسخ المهدى صلى الله عليه
واله الطاهر الطهر وعلى اصحابه الخير وازوجه امهات المومنين وعلى
التابعين وتابعى التابعين من الاولين والحسنى الى يوم الدين وبالله نستعين
نراى انفع كان بهذا الذى وفقك الله ولدوله والعلم شفاكر حسر جا
اناسلب ها طلبا لاحصار وعذرا كا عن المطالى والاكار لسهل على
برفسوا به ويل بان اسمعا البهوعاد والله وان وفقنا والحفظ
بالدنيا وهو حسادتم الوكل وناول ما بنداله ربدله ثم الامر الوقر

Introduction of Ibn Battah

بِسْمِ اللهِ الرَّحْمَنِ الرَّحِيمِ

The Shaikh, The Imām, Abū 'Abdillāh 'Ubaidillāh Ibn Muhammad Ibn Muhammad Hamdān Ibn Battah Al-'Ukbarī (رَحِمَهُ اللَّهُ):

Praise be to Allāh, who has poured upon us His blessings and made apparent to us His bounties. He has made from the best of them (i.e. these bounties), and most tremendous of them, His guiding us to knowing Him, and attesting to His lordship. He has made us from the followers of the correct religion, and from the party of the religion of truth.

Then to Him be praise, we praise and extol Him, due to that which He has bestowed upon us of guidance to Islām, and that He has taught us and granted us success to arrive at the Sunnah. He has inspired us with it and taught us that which we knew not. Indeed, the virtues of Allāh upon us have been great.

And may the peace and blessings of Allāh be upon Muhammad, His prophet, with whom He is pleased, and His chosen Messenger, (the one) He sent to establish His proofs and to affirm His oneness, and call to Him, with wisdom and good sermon.

And to Allāh is all praise for his (the Messenger's صَلَّى اللَّهُ عَلَيْهِ وَسَلَّمَ) manifest legislation, and pure Sunan and his noble mannerisms.

We seek the aid and success from Allāh in making correct statements, and in performing righteous action, and we ask that He makes our goal, the goal of what we have burdened ourselves with, nothing other than seeking His face, and giving precedence to His good pleasure and His love (over our own), that our striving may be accepted with Him, and that our reward with Him be abundant.

As for what follows:

Indeed, I ask Allāh that He bestows His success upon us, the like of which will open for us the doors of truthfulness, and will grant us protection from falling into pitfalls of error, and treading the slippery path of opinion, for indeed He is the mercy-giver, the loving, the one who continually does as He wills.

The Reason for Authoring the Book

Indeed, when I observed what has overcome the people, and what they have made manifest, that which has overpowered them and caused them to deem evil desires, false opinion, distortion of the Sunnah and substitution of the religion something good. To the extent that it has become a cause for their division, (a cause) for opening the door of trials, blindness of their hearts, splitting of their ranks and dividing their unity. They have thrown the book (of Allāh) behind their backs, and have taken the ignorant and the misguided, as lords in their affairs, after knowledge has come to them from their Lord.

They use (false) argumentation in that which they claim, and use the witness of conjecture as a definitive authority. Falsehood is proof for them in matters of their creed. They have blindly followed in their religion, those who have no knowledge, concerning affairs they have no evidence for in the book (of Allāh), neither do they have the proof of consensus. By Allāh, devils often put misguidance in the mouths of their heretical brothers, statements of heresy and newly invented innovations, embellished in beautified speech, innovated novelties that bring doubts to the hearts and minds. Trials that cause chests to tremor, that no human will stand up against, and whose quaking will cause no foot to remain firm, except he who Allāh protects through knowledge, and aids him with firmness, coupled with forbearance.

I collected in this book, a portion of that which I have heard, and something of that which we have transmitted from the Imāms of the religion, the great people of knowledge among the Muslims, that which they have conveyed to us from the Messenger of the Lord of all the worlds, and that which he has encouraged his followers from the believers with.

Likewise, that which he has commanded, from clinging to his Sunnah, and following his path, adhering to his guidance and traversing upon his way.

I have preceded this with a warning against deviation and censure of disparity, and (with) a mention of that which Allāh (عَزَّوَجَلَّ) has commanded His Messenger with, from clinging to the Jamā'ah and departing from the people of deviation, splitting and repulsive behaviour.

And that which is binding upon Ahlus-Sunnah from being distinct from those who oppose their creed, and break their covenant (with Allāh), defame their religion and intend to split their unity.

After which will follow an explanation of the Sunnah (taken from) the consensus of the Imāms and the agreement of the Ummah, and the unanimity of the people of faith.

I have gathered in this regard, that which no Muslim should be ignorant of, and Allāh — blessed be His name — will not excuse the one who neglects it, nor will He look at the one who opposes or defames it. His evidence (for his opposition) becomes feeble when he mocks the religion (with his innovation). His feet slipped when he criticized and spoke ill of the Imāms of the Muslims. He indeed was blinded from guidance when he opposed the Sunnah of Al-Mustafā (The Chosen One) and (opposed) the rightly guided ones.

So may the peace and blessings of Allāh be upon him (Muhammad) and his good and pure household, and upon his chosen companions, and his wives, who are the mothers of the believers, and upon those who follow them in righteousness, and their followers from the first and last generations until the day of judgement, and in Allāh, we seek aid!

Then I affirm here, in this book of mine, Oh My brother, — may Allāh grant you the success to accept and act upon it — texts I have (intentionally) left the mention of their chains of transmission seeking to make it concise, and in an attempt to avoid making it lengthy and burdensome. That it may be digestible for the one who reads it, and that the one who listens to it feels no fatigue and he is able to understand it.

Indeed Allāh is the patron of our success, and it is He who takes us by our hands, He is sufficient for us and the best disposer of our affairs.

Section One

The Ahādīth and Narrations that Indicate the Compulsory Nature of Clinging to the Sunnah, loving the Sahābah and the Dispraise of Innovation and Splitting in the Religion.

Thus, we will commence by mentioning the first affair, which is:

That which Allāh has commanded with, and mentioned in His book, the affair of clinging to the Jamā'ah and the prohibition against splitting and dividing.

Allāh — The Most High — says:

وَاعْتَصِمُوا بِحَبْلِ اللَّهِ جَمِيعًا وَلَا تَفَرَّقُوا

"Cling to the rope of Allāh together and do not be divided." — Sūrah Āli Imrān (3):103

He additionally threatened the one who splits from the Jamā'ah of the Muslims when He said:

وَلَا تَكُونُوا كَالَّذِينَ تَفَرَّقُوا وَاخْتَلَفُوا مِن بَعْدِ مَا جَاءَهُمُ الْبَيِّنَاتُ

وَأُولَئِكَ لَهُمْ عَذَابٌ عَظِيمٌ

"And do not be like those divided and differed after the clarification had come to them. For them is a painful punishment." — Sūrah Āli Imrān (3):105

Thus Allāh — blessed and exalted be He — has commanded with unity upon His religion and His obedience. He — The Mighty and Majestic — says:

$$وَمَا أُمِرُوا إِلَّا لِيَعْبُدُوا اللَّهَ مُخْلِصِينَ لَهُ الدِّينَ حُنَفَاءَ وَيُقِيمُوا الصَّلَاةَ$$

$$وَيُؤْتُوا الزَّكَاةَ ۚ وَذَٰلِكَ دِينُ الْقَيِّمَةِ$$

"Indeed they were not commanded except to worship Allāh, being sincere in religion to Him and to establish the prayer and to give the Zakāh and that is the upright religion." — SŪRAH AL-BAYYINAH (98):5

And He, The Most High, says:

$$إِنَّ اللَّهَ يُحِبُّ الَّذِينَ يُقَاتِلُونَ فِي سَبِيلِهِ صَفًّا كَأَنَّهُم بُنْيَانٌ مَّرْصُوصٌ$$

"Indeed, Allāh loves those who fight in His path in ranks as though they were a fortified structure." — SŪRAH AS-SAFF (61):4

Refraining From Those who Oppose the Belief of Ahlus-Sunnah

In addition, (we will mention) that which the believers have been commanded with, from separating from those who break their contracts, and who breach their covenants, and speak ill of their religion, (we have been commanded to) stay away from them, and to abandon sitting with them, and listening to their errors and addresses.

Thus Allāh — The Most High — says:

$$وَقَدْ نَزَّلَ عَلَيْكُمْ فِي الْكِتَابِ أَنْ إِذَا سَمِعْتُمْ آيَاتِ اللَّهِ يُكْفَرُ بِهَا وَيُسْتَهْزَأُ$$

$$بِهَا فَلَا تَقْعُدُوا مَعَهُمْ حَتَّىٰ يَخُوضُوا فِي حَدِيثٍ غَيْرِهِ ۚ إِنَّكُمْ إِذًا مِّثْلُهُمْ ۗ إِنَّ اللَّهَ$$

$$جَامِعُ الْمُنَافِقِينَ وَالْكَافِرِينَ فِي جَهَنَّمَ جَمِيعًا$$

And it has already been revealed to you in the book (this Qur'ān) that when you hear the verses of Allāh being denied and mocked at, then sit not with them, until they engage in a talk other than that; (but if you stayed with them) certainly, in that case, you would be like them. Surely, Allāh will collect the hypocrites and disbelievers all together in Hell." — SŪRAH AN NISĀ' (4):140

....

[١] - وَأَمَرَ رَسُولُ اللَّهِ (صَلَّى ٱللَّهُ عَلَيْهِ وَسَلَّمَ) الثَّلاَثَةِ الَّذِينَ تَخَلَّفُوا عَنْهُ بِهُجْرَانِهِم وُمُبَايَنَتِهِم

وَأَمَرَهُـم أَنْ يَعْتَزِلُوا نِسَاءَهُم حَتَّى أَنْزَلَ اللَّهُ - عز وجل - تَوْبَتَهُم

1 — The Messenger (صَلَّى ٱللَّهُ عَلَيْهِ وَسَلَّمَ) commanded that the three who were absent from the battle (of Tabūk) be boycotted and ostracised and he commanded them to stay away from their wives until Allāh revealed (to His Messenger) the acceptance of their repentance.

•

[٢] - وقـال (صَلَّى ٱللَّهُ عَلَيْهِ وَسَلَّمَ) «أَوَّلَ مـا دَخَـلَ النَّقْصُ عَلَى بَنِي إِسْرَائِيلَ كَانَ الرَّجُـلُ

يَلْقَى أَخَاهُ فَيَقُولُ يَا هَذَا اتَّقِ اللَّهِ وَدَعْ مَا تَصْنَعُ فَإِنَّهُ لاَ يَحِلُّ لَكَ ثُمَّ يَلْقَاهُ

مِـنَ الْغَـدِ فَلاَ يَمْنَعُهُ ذَلِكَ أَنْ يَكُـونَ أَكِيلَـهُ وَشَرِيبَهُ وَقَعِيـدَهُ فَلَمَّـا فَعَلُـوا ذَلِـكَ

ضَرَبَ اللَّهُ قُلُوبَ بَعْضِهِمْ بِبَعْضٍ». - ثُمَّ قَالَ: «لُعِنَ الَّذِينَ كَفَرُوا مِـن بَنِي

إِسْرَائِيلَ عَلَى لِسَانِ دَاوُودَ وَعِيسَى ابْنِ مَرْيَم» {المائدة: ٧٨} إِلَى قَوْلِهِ «وَلَـوْ

كَانُوا يُؤْمِنُونَ بِاللَّهِ وَالنَّبِيِّ وَمَا أُنزِلَ إِلَيْهِ مَا اتَّخَذُوهُـم أَوْلِيَاءَ وَلَكِنَّ كَثِيرًا مِّنهُمْ

فَاسِقُونَ» {المائدة: ٨١}

2 — He (صَلَّى ٱللَّهُ عَلَيْهِ وَسَلَّمَ) said: "Indeed, the beginning of degradation among the children of Isrā'īl was that a man would meet a man and say: 'Oh You! Fear Allāh! And leave alone that which you are doing for indeed it is not permissible for you!'

Then he would meet him the following day and that would not prevent him from eating, drinking and sitting with him. When

they did this Allāh turned their hearts one against another." Then
he said (quoting the Qur'anic verse): *"Those among the children of
Isrā'īl who disbelieved were cursed upon the tongue of Dāwūd and Īsā the
son of Maryam..."* [SŪRAH AL-MĀ'IDAH (5): 81] up to His statement:
*"And had they believed in Allāh and the Prophet (Muhammad) never would
they have taken them as awliyā' (protectors and helpers) but many of them
are fāsiqūn (disobedient to Allāh, rebellious)."* [SŪRAH AL-MĀ'IDAH
(5): 81] [1]

•

[٣] - وقال (صَلَّى اللَّهُ عَلَيْهِ وَسَلَّمَ): مَثَلُ الْقَائِمِ عَلَى حُدُودِ اللَّهِ وَالْمُدْهِنِ فِيهَا، كَمَثَلِ
قَوْمٍ اسْتَهَمُوا عَلَى سَفِينَةٍ فِي الْبَحْرِ فَأَصَابَ بَعْضُهُمْ أَسْفَلَهَا وَبَعْضُهُمْ أَعْلَاهَا
وَكَانَ الَّذِينَ فِي أَسْفَلِهَا يَخْرُجُونَ فَيَسْتَقُونَ الْمَاءَ وَيَصُبُّونَ عَلَى الَّذِينَ أَعْلَاهَا
فَيُؤْذُونَهُمْ فَقَالُوا: لَا نَدَعُكُمْ تَمُرُّونَ عَلَيْنَا فَتُؤْذُونَنَا فَقَالَ الَّذِينَ فِي أَسْفَلِهَا أَمَّا إِذْ
مَنَعْتُمُونَا فَنَنْقُبُ السَّفِينَةَ مِنْ أَسْفَلِهَا وَنَسْتَقِي، قَالَ: فَإِنْ أَخَذُوا عَلَى أَيْدِيهِمْ
فَمَنَعُوهُمْ نَجَوْا جَمِيعًا، وَإِنْ تَرَكُوهُمْ هَلَكُوا جَمِيعًا.

3 — He (صَلَّى اللَّهُ عَلَيْهِ وَسَلَّمَ) also said: "The example of the one who
establishes the boundaries of Allāh (i.e. enjoins the good and forbids
the evil) and the one who falls into them is as the example of a
people who drew lots upon a ship at sea (in order to decide who
should take the upper or lower decks), so some were allocated the
lower deck and some the upper deck.

Those who were on the lower deck would (come up), go out and
take water (from outside the boat) and pour it upon those on the
upper deck. They (i.e. those on the upper deck) responded to them
saying *'We are not going to let you come to us (with this water) and harm
us! (and make the ship heavy)!'*

---

1 — Collected by Ahmad (1/391) and Abū Dāwūd (4336) and Ibn Mājah (4006) Shaikh
Al-Albānī declared it *'da'īf'* (weak) in *Ad-Da'īfah* (1105).

Those in the lower deck said: *'If you are going to prevent us (i.e. from getting water) then we will make a hole in the bottom of the boat and take the water [that way]!'* If they take them by the hand and stop them they will all be saved, but if they leave them they will all be destroyed!"[1]

The Blameworthy Nature of Differing, and the Encouragement to Follow the Sunnah and be United

[٤] - وقال (صَلَّى ٱللَّٰهُ عَلَيْهِ وَسَلَّمَ): افْتَرَقَتْ بَنُو إِسْرَائِيلَ عَلَى ثِنْتَيْنِ وَسَبْعِينَ فِرْقَةً وَسَتَفْتَرِقُ أُمَّتِي عَلَى ثَلَاثٍ وَسَبْعِينَ فِرْقَةً فِرْقَة نَاجِيَة وَثِنْتَيْن وَسَبْعِين فِي النَّارِ.

4 — He (صَلَّى ٱللَّٰهُ عَلَيْهِ وَسَلَّمَ) also said: "The Children of Isrā'īl split into seventy-two sects and my Ummah shall split into seventy-three sects, one sect will be saved and seventy-two will be in the fire."[2]

---

1 — Collected by Al-Bukhārī (2493) upon the authority of An-Nu'mān Ibn Bashīr.

2 — Collected by Abū Dāwūd (4596), At-Tirmidhī (2640) Ibn Mājah (3991) and both wordings [ONE] *'They are the main body...'* and [TWO] *'They are those who are upon that which I and my companions are upon...'* are declared *'sahih'* by Shaikh Al-Albānī in *As-Sahihah* (203, 204). He also responds to those from the people of desires who attempt to declare it weak (in particular the version with the addition wording *'they are those who are upon that which I and my companions are upon today'*) with a number of responses, the summary of which is as follows:

i.   The application of the knowledge-based sciences of hadīth and criticism (upon the hadīth's chains of narration), necessitates accepting this additional wording. Therefore, there is no consideration, for the statement of the one who declares it weak.

ii. Those who authenticate it are greater in number and more knowledgeable in hadīth than Ibn Hazm (who is from those whose speech is relied upon in declaring it weak) especially since he is well known with the people of knowledge for being harsh in criticism. As for Ibnul-Wazīr (a well-known Yemeni scholar who the deviant Al-Kawthari relies upon), then his criticism did not revolve around the chain of narration but rather the meaning, and since that is the case, then it is not possible for anyone to make a definitive statement based upon this, especially when it is possible to reconcile the meaning found in the other wordings.

iii. Ibnul-Wazīr also authenticates the hadīth himself in his book *Ar-Rawdh Al-Bāsim*.

iv. Another great scholar from Yemen, Shaikh Sālih Al-Muqbili subliminally responds to the issues posed by Ibnul Wazīr in his book *Al-Alamush-Shāmikh* p. 414 wherein he says: "The hadīth concerning the splitting of the Ummah into 73 sects, has

[٥] - وقال (صَلَّالَلَهُعَلَيْهِوَسَلَّمَ): عَلَيْكُمْ بِسُنَّتِي وَسُنَّةِ الْخُلَفَاءِ الرَّاشِدِينَ مِنْ بَعْدِي، عَضُّوا عَلَيْهَا بِالنَّوَاجِذِ.

5 — He (صَلَّالَلَهُعَلَيْهِوَسَلَّمَ) also said: "Cling to my Sunnah, and the Sunnah of the rightly guided caliphs after me, hold onto that with your molar teeth."[1]

•

[٦] - وَقَالَ (صَلَّالَلَهُعَلَيْهِوَسَلَّمَ): لَقَدْ جِئْتُكُمْ بِهَا بَيْضَاءَ نَقِيَّةً فَلَا تَخْتَلِفُوا بَعْدِي.

6 — He (صَلَّالَلَهُعَلَيْهِوَسَلَّمَ) also said: "Indeed I have come to you with that which is pure and white, so do not differ after me."[2]

•

[٧] - وَقَالَ (صَلَّالَلَهُعَلَيْهِوَسَلَّمَ): قَدْ تَرَكْتُكُمْ عَلَى الوَاضِحَةِ؛ فَلَا تَذْهَبُوا يَمِينًا، وَلَا شِمَالًا.

7 — He (صَلَّالَلَهُعَلَيْهِوَسَلَّمَ) also said: "Indeed I have left you upon clarity, so do not veer left or right."[3]

---

numerous versions that support each other in such a way that there can be no doubt concerning what it indicates of meaning." (Abbreviated from Silsilatul Ahādīthis Sahihah: hadīth 204)

1 — Collected by Ahmad (4/126) Abū Dāwūd (3607) At-Tirmidhī (2676) and Ibn Mājah (42) Ad Dārimī (95) Al-Lillakā'ī (1/74-75) and was declared 'sahīh' by Al-Albānī in Sahīh Ibn Mājah (As-Sahīlhah: 937)

2 — Collected by Ahmad 3/338 and Al-Baghawī (1/270) but without the words: "...so do not differ after me." Al-Haythamī in Majma' Az-Zawā'id (1/174) attributed it to Abī Ya'lā and Al-Bazzār and then said "In it (i.e. in its chain of narration) is Mujālid Ibn Sa'īd and Imām Ahmad declared him weak." Shaikh Al-Albānī declared it 'hasan' based upon supporting chains of narration in Takhrīj Al-Mishkāt (1/63).

3 — Collected by Ibn Mājah (5) with the wording: "Upon the like of which is clear and white its night and its day are the same." Declared 'hasan' by Al-Albānī in Sahīh Ibn Mājah (5). As for the wording mentioned here, then it is attributed to 'Umar as his statement and not a hadīth of the Prophet (صَلَّالَلَهُعَلَيْهِوَسَلَّمَ). 'Umar gave a khutbah and said: "'Oh People! I have laid down for you Sunan, and have established for you compulsory

[٨] - وقال (صَلَّى ٱللَّهُ عَلَيْهِ وَسَلَّمَ): إِنَّ ٱللَّهَ لَيُدْخِلُ الْعَبْدَ الْجَنَّةَ بِالسُّنَّةِ يَتَمَسَّكُ بِهَا.

8 — He (صَلَّى ٱللَّهُ عَلَيْهِ وَسَلَّمَ) also said: "Indeed Allāh will let His servant into Jannah by way of His holding onto the Sunnah."[1]

•

[٩] - وقال (صَلَّى ٱللَّهُ عَلَيْهِ وَسَلَّمَ): وَاللَّهِ لَوْ أَنَّ مُوسَى وعِيسَى حَيَّانِ؛ لِمَا حَلَّ لَهُمَا إِلَّا أن يَتَّبِعَانِي.

9 — He (صَلَّى ٱللَّهُ عَلَيْهِ وَسَلَّمَ) also said: "By Allāh! If Mūsā and 'Īsā were both alive, then they would have no choice but to follow me."[2]

The Prohibition Against Argumentation in Religion

[١٠] - وخَرَجَ (صَلَّى ٱللَّهُ عَلَيْهِ وَسَلَّمَ) وَهُمْ يَتَنَازَعُونَ فِي الْقَدَرِ فقال: بِهَذَا أُمِرْتُمْ أَوْ لَيْسَ عَنْ هَذَا نُهِيتُمْ؟! إِنَّمَا هَلَكَ مَنْ كَانَ قَبْلَكُمْ بِتَمَارِيهِمْ فِي دِينِهِمْ.

10 — He (صَلَّى ٱللَّهُ عَلَيْهِ وَسَلَّمَ) came out (from his abode) and they (some of his companions) were arguing about Qadr (Pre decree) so he said: "Is this what you have been commanded with?! Have you not been

---

matters and have left you upon clarity, except if you stray with the people left and right' — then he struck one of his hands with the other." Collected by Imām Mālik in *Al-Muwatta'* (2383) with an authentic chain of narration.

1 — Collected by Ad-Dāraqutnī in *Atrāful Gharā'ib wal-Afrād* (6146) and declared 'weak'. It was also collected by Ibn Battah in *Al-Ibānatul Kubrā* (51) and Al-Harawī in *Dhammul-Kalām* (702) upon the authority of Anas and Al-Lillakā'ī (8) similarly upon the authority of Anas with the wording: *"Whoever brings life to my Sunnah has loved me and whoever loves me then he will be with me in Jannah."* That which bears witness to the correctness of its meaning is the statement of the Prophet (صَلَّى ٱللَّهُ عَلَيْهِ وَسَلَّمَ): *"Whoever obeys me will enter Jannah."* Collected by Al-Bukhārī (7280).

2 — This statement of the Prophet is the end of Hadīth No. 6, though the mention of 'Īsā does not occur in any of its wordings.

prohibited from this?! Certainly, those who were before you were destroyed due to them arguing about their religion."[1]

The Blameworthy Nature of Disputing About the Qur'ān Specifically, and the Dispraise of the one Who Does So

[١١] - وَخَرَجَ (صَلَّى اللهُ عَلَيْهِ وَسَلَّمَ) يَوْمًا عَلَى أَصْحَابِهِ وَهُمْ يَقُولُونَ أَلَمْ يَقُلِ اللَّهُ كَذَا وَكَذَا يَرُدُّ بعضُهم عَلَى بَعْضٍ فَكَأَنَّمَا فُقِئَ فِي وَجْهِهِ حَبُّ الرُّمَّانِ فَقَالَ: إِنَّمَا أَفْسَدَ عَلَى الأُمَمِ هـذا فَلَا تَضْرِبُوا كِتَابَ اللَّهِ بَعْضَهُ بِبَعْضٍ فَإِنَّ ذَلِكَ يُوقِعُ الشَّكَّ فِي قُلُوبِكُمْ.

11 — He (صَلَّى اللهُ عَلَيْهِ وَسَلَّمَ) came out to his companions one day and they were saying: *'Didn't Allāh say such and such?'* And they were responding one to another. (When that occurred) it was as though someone had thrown pomegranate seeds in his face (i.e. his face had reddened) then he said: "Indeed the previous nations became corrupt due to this! Do not rebut the book of Allāh with the book of Allāh! For certainly that will cast doubt in your hearts."[2]

---

1 — Collected by Ahmad (2/181) Ibn Mājah (85) upon the authority of 'Abdullāh Ibn 'Amr with slightly variant wording: "He (صَلَّى اللهُ عَلَيْهِ وَسَلَّمَ) came out (from his abode) and they (some of his companions) were arguing about Qadr (Pre-Decree) so he said: 'Is this what you have been commanded with?! Is this why you were created?! Rebutting the book of Allāh with the book of Allāh?! It was due to this, the previous nations were destroyed.'" Declared 'hasan-sahīh' by Al-Albānī in *Sahīh Sunan Ibn Mājah* (85).

Benefit of the hadīth: This hadīth and the one that follows, indicates that the religion is based upon *ittibā'* (following the texts). We refrain from speaking about affairs we do not understand using our intellect. The book of Allāh does not contradict itself. Unclear verses are understood in the light of clear verses and in the light of the Sunnah as understood by the Sahābah.

2 — This is a variant version of the previous hadīth collected by Al-Lillakā'ī (1/115) and Ahmad (2/195) Declared 'sahīh' by Al-Albānī in *Sharh At-Tahāwiyah* (p. 288). As for the statement: *"For certainly that will cast doubt in your hearts,"* then this does not occur in the various versions of the hadīth. However, it is established as a statement of Ibn 'Abbās, collected by Al-Harawī in *Dhammul-Kalām* (171). Thus Hāfidh Ibn Hajr mentions in *Fat-hul-Bārī* (9/100-101) "It is present in the collection of Ibn Abī Shaibah from the

[١٢] - وقال (صَلَّى اللهُ عَلَيْهِ وَسَلَّمَ): لا تُجَالِسُوا أَهْلَ القَدَرِ فَإِنَّهُمْ الَّذِينَ يَخُوضُونَ فِي آيَاتِ اللَّهِ - عَزَّ وَجَلَّ.

12 — He (صَلَّى اللهُ عَلَيْهِ وَسَلَّمَ) also said: "Do not sit with the people of Qadr (a people who have gone astray in regard to the belief in pre-decree) for indeed they are the ones who have entered into false speech about the verses of Allāh."[1]

•

[١٣] - وقال (صَلَّى اللهُ عَلَيْهِ وَسَلَّمَ): المِرَاءَ فِي القُرآنِ كُفْرٌ.

13 — He (صَلَّى اللهُ عَلَيْهِ وَسَلَّمَ) also said: "Arguing and debating concerning the Qur'ān is disbelief."[2]

Affirmation that the Qur'ān is the speech of Allāh

[١٤] - وقال (صَلَّى اللهُ عَلَيْهِ وَسَلَّمَ): إِنَّكُمْ لَا تَرْجِعُونَ إِلَى اللَّهِ بِشَيْءٍ أَفْضَلَ مِمَّا خَرَجَ مِنْهُ - يَعْنِي: القُرْآنَ.

---

statement of Ibn 'Abbās: "Do not rebut the book of Allāh with the book of Allāh! For certainly that will cast doubt in your hearts."

1 — Collected by Ahmad (1/30) and Abū Dāwūd (4710,4720) and Hākim (1/159) with the variant wording: "Do not sit with the people of Qadr and do not open up debate with them" — declared 'weak' by Shaikh Al-Albānī In Dha'īf Al-Jāmi' (6193).

Benefit of the hadīth: The hadīth indicates that those who have gone astray in relation to issues of creed, then the creed is to be explained to them. We pay no attention to their opinion when it opposes that which is clear. We are not interested in the opinions that oppose clear creed. The affair is to be explained to him, if he is obstinate and persists, then we do not sit with them or take them as companions.

2 — Collected by At-Tabarānī in Al-Mu'jamul-Kabīr (496), Abū Dāwūd (4603) and declared 'hasan-sahīh' by Al-Albānī in Sahīh Sunan Abī Dāwūd (4603).

Benefit of the hadīth: Arguing concerning the Qur'ān may be major kufr or minor kufr. If the argument involves rejection of that which the Qur'ān clearly indicates, then it is major kufr.

14 — He (صَلَّاللَّهُعَلَيْهِوَسَلَّمَ) also said: "Indeed you will not return back to Allāh with anything better than that which has come from Him (i.e. the Qur'ān)."[1]

•

[١٥] - وقال (صَلَّاللَّهُعَلَيْهِوَسَلَّمَ): إِنَّ قُرَيْشًا مَنَعَتْنِي أَنْ أُبَلِّغَ كَلَامَ رَبِّي.

15 — He (صَلَّاللَّهُعَلَيْهِوَسَلَّمَ) also said: "Indeed Quraish has prevented me from conveying the speech of my Lord."[2]

•

[١٦] - وقال (صَلَّاللَّهُعَلَيْهِوَسَلَّمَ) لِجَابِرٍ: أَعَلِمْتَ أَنَّ اللَّهَ أَحْيَا أَبَاكَ فَكَلَّمَهُ كِفَاحًا.

16 — He (صَلَّاللَّهُعَلَيْهِوَسَلَّمَ) also said to Jābir: "Do you know that Allāh has given life to your father and has spoken to him directly."[3]

---

1 — Collected by Imām Ahmad in *Az-Zuhd* (1/35) Al-Baihaqī in *Al-Asmā' was Sifāt* (503) by 'Abdullāh Ibn Ahmad in *As-Sunnah* (1/140) Al-Hākim In his *Mustadrak* (1/741) Shaikh Al-Albānī had authenticated the hadīth in *As-Sahīhah* (961) then later declared it 'weak' in *Adh-Dha'īfah* (1957) and that was his final verdict upon it.

Benefit of the hadīth: The hadīth indicates that the best thing a believer can do is memorise the Qur'ān and act upon it. It similarly indicates that false interpretation of the Qur'ān causes the believer to abandon true action upon it, since acting upon false interpretation is, in essence, acting upon other than the Qur'ān.

2 — Collected by Ahmad (3/390) and Abū Dāwūd (4734) and declared 'sahīh' by Shaikh Al-Albānī in *Sahīh Sunan Abī Dāwūd* (4734).

Benefit of the hadīth: The hadīth indicates that the Qur'ān is truly the speech of Allāh and not an 'expression' or 'representation' of His speech.

3 — This refers to the following hadīth: Jābir Ibn 'Abdullāh said: "The Messenger of Allāh met me on an occasion and said to me: *'Why is it I see you upset?'* So I said: *'Indeed my father was Martyred and killed on the day of Uhud and he left behind him dependants and debt.'* So he said: *'Should I not inform you of what your father met Allāh with?'* I said: *'Of course Oh Messenger of Allāh!'* He said: *'Indeed Allāh has never spoken to anyone except from behind a veil, but He gave your father life and spoke to him directly. He said:*

| "Oh my servant do you wish that I should give you anything?"

He said: "Oh my Lord! I wish you would give me life and let me be killed in your way a second time!"

He said:

[١٧] - وقال (صَلَّى ٱللَّهُ عَلَيْهِ وَسَلَّمَ): يَكُونُ بَعْدِي فِتْنَة يُصْبِحُ الرَّجُلُ فِيهَا مُؤْمِناً وَيُمْسِي

كَافِراً، وَيُمْسِي مُؤْمِناً وَيُصْبِحُ كَافِراً، إِلَّا مَنْ أَحْيَاهُ اللَّهُ بِالعِلْمِ.

17 — He (صَلَّى ٱللَّهُ عَلَيْهِ وَسَلَّمَ) also said: "There will be afflictions after me.
During which a man will be a believer in the morning, and see his
evening a disbeliever. He will be a believer in the evening[1] and see
his morning a disbeliever, except the one who Allāh gives life to
through knowledge."

The Command to Follow Abū Bakr and ʿUmar

[١٨] - وَقَالَ (صَلَّى ٱللَّهُ عَلَيْهِ وَسَلَّمَ): «اقْتَدُوا بِاللَّذَيْنِ مِنْ بَعْدِي: أَبِي بَكْرٍ وَعُمَرَ» رضي

اللَّه عنهما.

18 — He (صَلَّى ٱللَّهُ عَلَيْهِ وَسَلَّمَ) also said: "Follow the two that come after me:
Abū Bakr and ʿUmar."[2]

"Indeed it has already preceded from me that they will not return to it (i.e. this
world).'"

And this verse was revealed: 'Think not of those who are killed in the way of Allāh as
dead...'" [SŪRAH ĀLI ʿIMRĀN (3): 168]

(Collected by At Tirmidhi (3010) and declared 'hasan' by Shaikh Al-Albānī.)

Benefit of the hadīth: The hadīth indicates that Allāh actually speaks and that His speech
is not metaphoric.

1 — Collected by Ibn Mājah (3954) and Ad-Dārimī (338) and At-Tabarānī in Al-Kabīr
(7910) and declared 'very weak' by Shaikh Al-Albānī Dha'īf Ibn Mājah (3954). The
popular version of this hadīth is authentic and occurs in Sahīh Muslim with the wording:
"Hasten to the performance of good deeds, for there will be trials like the portion of a
dark night. A man will wake in the morning a believer and see his evening a disbeliever.
He will be a believer in the evening and a disbeliever by the morning, he will sell his
religion for a worldly gain." Collected by Muslim (118).

2 — Collected by Ahmad (5/382) and At-Tirmidhī (3662) and declared 'sahīh' by
Shaikh Al-Albānī in Sahīhul Jāmiʿ (1142)

Benefit of the hadīth: After the Imām mentioned the hadīth concerning fitan, this
hadīth indicates that safety from afflictions is in following the companions, at the head of
them Abū Bakr and ʿUmar – (رَضِيَ ٱللَّهُ عَنْهُمَا).

The Dispraise of Relying Upon Opinion and Abandoning the Sunan

[١٩] - وقال (ﷺ): لَمْ يَزَلْ أَمْرُ بَنِي إِسْرَائِيلَ مُعْتَدِلًا حَتَّى نَشَأَ فِيهِمُ الْمُوَلَّدُونَ، وَأَبْنَاءُ سَبَايَا الْأُمَمِ فَأَخَذُوا بِالرَّأْيِ وَتَرَكُوا السُّنَنَ.

19 — He (ﷺ) also said: "The affair of the children of Isrā'īl did not cease to be upright until there grew among them the 'Muwalladūn', the children of prisoners of war of different nations, so they followed opinion and left the Sunan."[1]

The Blameworthy Nature of giving Islamic verdicts without Knowledge

[٢٠] - وقال (ﷺ): إِنَّ اللَّهَ لاَ يَنْزِعُ الْعِلْمَ انْتِزَاعًا مِنْ صُدُورِ الرِّجَالِ وَلَكِنْ يَقْبِضُ العِلْمَ بِقَبْضِ الْعُلَمَاءِ حَتَّى لَمْ يَبْقَ عَالِمًا، اتَّخَذَ النَّاسُ رُؤَسَاءَ جُهَّالًا، فَسُئِلُوا فَأَفْتَوْا بِغَيْرِ عِلْمٍ، فَضَلُّوا، وَأَضَلُّوا.

20 — He (ﷺ) said: "Indeed Allāh will not take knowledge by removing it from the breasts of men, but He will take knowledge through the death of the scholars, until there is not a scholar left, then the people take for themselves ignorant leaders, so they will ask them and they will give verdicts without knowledge, thus they will go astray and lead others astray."[2]

---

1 — Collected by Ibn Mājah (56) with the wording: "The affair of the children of Isrā'īl has not ceased to be upright until there grew among them the 'Muwalladūn', the children of prisoners of war of different nations, so they followed opinion and went astray and lead others astray." Declared 'weak' by Shaikh Al-Albānī in Dha'īf Ibn Mājah (56).

Benefit of the hadīth: The hadīth indicates the evil effect of external influence in the affairs of the religion (not the worldly affairs). This was one of the causes of the misguidance of the Children of Isrā'īl.

2 — Collected by Ahmad (2/190) and Ibn Mājah (52) and declared 'sahīh' by Shaikh Al-Albānī in Sahīhul-Jāmi' (1854).

The Prohibition Against Abundant Questioning

[٢١] - وَنَهَى (صَلَّىٱللَّهُعَلَيْهِوَسَلَّمَ) عَن قِيلَ وقَالَ وإِضَاعَةِ المَالِ، وكَثْرَةِ السُّؤَال

21 — He (صَلَّىٱللَّهُعَلَيْهِوَسَلَّمَ) prohibited: Gossiping (he say, she say), wasting wealth and excessive questioning.[1]

•

[٢٢] - وَكَانَ (صَلَّىٱللَّهُعَلَيْهِوَسَلَّمَ) يَكْرَهُ كَثْرَةَ الْمَسَائِلِ وَنَهَى (صَلَّىٱللَّهُعَلَيْهِوَسَلَّمَ) عَنِ الْغُلُوطَاتِ وَقِيلَ هِيَ شِدَادُ الْمَسَائِلِ وَصُعَابِها

22 — He (صَلَّىٱللَّهُعَلَيْهِوَسَلَّمَ) prohibited excessive querying and *ghulūtāt*.[2] It is said[3] this refers to difficult and troublesome questioning.

•

[٢٣] - وقال (صَلَّىٱللَّهُعَلَيْهِوَسَلَّمَ): اتْرُكُونِي مَا تَرَكْتُكُمْ.

23 — He (صَلَّىٱللَّهُعَلَيْهِوَسَلَّمَ) said: "Do not cross-question me in regards to what I have left you with."[4]

•

Benefit of the hadīth: The hadīth indicates the great station of the scholars of the religion. It also indicates that following the ignorant, those who have not taken their knowledge from its carriers, is a great door to misguidance.

1 — Collected by Al-Bukhārī (1477) and Muslim (115). Benefit of the hadīth: The hadīth indicates the evil effect of gossiping and that it causes one to fall into error. This, alongside unnecessary excessive questioning is a common trait among the people of innovation and deviation.

2 — Some scholars hold that *'ghulūtāt'* refers to questioning that causes a person to fall into error.

3 — This explanation has been attributed to Imām Al-Awzā'i. Collected by Abū Dāwūd (3656) and At-Tabarānī in *Mu'jamul-Kabīr* (19/380) and declared weak by Al-Albānī in *Sahīh Sunan Abī Dāwūd* (3656).

4 — Collected by Al-Bukhārī (7288) and Muslim (3236). Benefit of the hadīth: The hadīth indicates the command to learn the religion and follow it, and to leave alone cross-questioning concerning issues that are clear.

[٢٤] - وقال (ﷺ): أَعْظَمُ الْمُسْلِمِينَ جُرْمًا مَنْ سَأَلَ عَنْ أمرٍ لَمْ يُحَرَّمْ فَحُرِّمَ مِنْ أَجْلِ مَسْأَلَتِهِ.

24 — He (ﷺ) said "The greatest of the Muslims in crime (against the Muslims) is the one who asks about something that wasn't made prohibited, then it was made prohibited due to his questioning."[1]

Dispraise For the People of Innovation and Those Who Accommodate Them

[٢٥] - وقال: «مَنْ أَحْدَثَ حَدَثًا، أَوْ آوَى مُحْدِثًا فَعَلَيْهِ لَعْنَةُ اللَّهِ وَلَعْنَةُ اللَّاعِنِينَ وَالْمَلَائِكَةِ وَالنَّاسِ أَجْمَعِينَ، لَا يَقْبَلُ اللَّهُ مِنْهُ صَرْفًا وَلَا عَدْلًا» فَقَالُوا لِلْحَسَنِ: مَا الْحَدَثُ؟ فَقَالَ: أَصْحَابُ الْفِتَنِ كُلُّهُم مُحْدِثُون، وَأَهْلُ الْأَهْواءِ كُلُّهُنَّ مُحْدِثُون.

25 — He (ﷺ) said: "Whosoever brings about an innovation, or accommodates an innovator, then upon him is the curse of Allāh and the curse of those who curse and the angels and all of the people. No form of repentance will be accepted from him nor ransom."[2] It was said to Al-Hasan (Al-Basri): *"What is Al-Hadath (a newly invented affair)?"*

---

1 — Collected by Al-Bukhārī (7289) and Muslim (2358) upon the authority of Sa'd Ibn Abī Waqqās.

Benefit of the hadīth: The hadīth indicates the prohibited nature of excessive cross-questioning about difficult issues that may cause harm to others. Some of the people of knowledge hold that this is in reference to the era of the Prophet (ﷺ), and that the questioning of the one who seeks guidance and understanding after his death is permissible.

2 — Collected by Abū Dāwūd (4530) and An-Nasā'ī (6911, 6912) and At-Tirmidhī (2127) with the wording: "Al-Madīnah is a sanctity from (Mount) 'Ayr to (Mount) Thowr, whosoever brings about an innovation in it, or accommodates an innovator, then upon him is the curse of Allāh and the curse of those who curse and the angels and all of the people. No form of repentance will be accepted from him nor ransom."

He responded: "The people of fitan (trials and afflictions in religion) are all people who bring about newly invented matters, and the people of desires are all individuals who bring about newly invented matters."

•

[٢٦] - وقال (صَلَّىٱللَّهُعَلَيْهِوَسَلَّمَ): كِلَابُ النَّارِ أَهْلِ ٱلْبِدَعِ.

26 — He (صَلَّىٱللَّهُعَلَيْهِوَسَلَّمَ) said: "The people of innovation are the dogs of the hellfire."[1]

•

[٢٧] - وقال (صَلَّىٱللَّهُعَلَيْهِوَسَلَّمَ): مَنْ وَقَّرَ صَاحِبَ بِدْعَةٍ فَقَدْ أَعَانَ عَلَى هَدْمِ

ٱلْإِسْلَامِ.

Declared 'sahīh' by Al-Albānī in Irwā' (1058). These two words صَرْفًا وَلَا عَدْلًا have also been explained by some scholars to mean that Allāh will not accept from him compulsory or supererogatory actions.

Benefit of the hadīth: The hadīth indicates a warning against innovation and accommodating innovators.

1 — Collected by Ibnul-Banā in Ar-Radd 'alal-Mubtadi'ah (1/3) and Abū Hātim Al-Khuzā'i in his Juz' (As occurs in Kanzul 'Umāl (1093) and declared 'dha'īf' by Shaikh Al-Albānī in Adh-Dha'īfah (2792). That which is well known is that the Prophet made this statement concerning the Khawārij as occurs in his statement "The Khawārij are the dogs of hellfire" — collected by Ibn Mājah (173) and Al-Ājjuri in Ash-Sharī'ah (35) and declared 'sahīh' by Al-Albānī in Sahīhul Jāmi' (3347). There is a narration attributed to Abū Umāmah wherein he said: كُنَّا نُسَمِّي أَصْحَابَ الأَهْوَاءِ كِلَابَ النَّار — "We used to refer to the people of desires as the dogs of hellfire." Collected by At-Tabarāni In Mu'jam Al-Kabīr (8/270). From the Salaf were those who used to refer to all of the people of desires as Khawārij such as Ayyūb As-Sikhtiyānī. Al-Firyābī narrates in Al-Qadr (375) the statement of Salām Ibn Abī Mutī' who said: "Ayyūb used to refer to all of the people of bid'ah as Khawārij and he would say 'The Khawārij differ in name but unite upon the sword.'" (See Dhammul-Hawā: 5/183 and Mu'jam Al-Kabīr of At-Tabarānī: 7/312)

Benefit of the hadīth: The hadīth indicates that since innovation is worse than major sin, and major sinners are under the threat of punishment, the people of innovation are either upon an innovation that constitutes disbelief or one that constitutes a sin greater than the major sins.

27 — He (ﷺ) said: "Whosoever honours a person of Innovation, then he has aided in the destruction of Islām!"[1]

•

[٢٨] - وَقَالَ ابْنُ مَسْعُودٍ - خَطَّ لَنَا رَسُولُ اللَّهِ (ﷺ) يَوْمًا خَطًّا ثُمَّ قَالَ: «هَذَا سَبِيلُ اللَّهِ»، ثُمَّ خَطَّ خُطُوطًا عَنْ يَمِينِ الخَطِّ وَيَسَارِهِ قَالَ: «هَذِهِ سُبُلٌ عَلَى كُلِّ سَبِيلٍ مِنْهَا شَيْطَانٌ يَدْعُو إِلَيْهِ»، ثُمَّ تَلَا: «وَأَنَّ هَذَا صِرَاطِي مُسْتَقِيمًا فَاتَّبِعُوهُ وَلَا تَتَّبِعُوا السُّبُلَ فَتَفَرَّقَ بِكُمْ عَن سَبِيلِهِ» {الأنعام: ١٥٣} يَعْنِي الْخُطُوطَ الَّتِي عَنْ يَمِينِهِ وَيَسَارِهِ.

28 — 'Abdullāh Ibn Mas'ūd said: "The Messenger of Allāh (ﷺ) drew a line for us in the sand one day and said: 'This is the path of Allāh,' then he drew lines to the right and to the left of it and said: 'These are the (divergent) paths, at the head of each one of them there is a shaytān calling to it,' then he recited (the statement of Allāh): 'Then this is my straightway so follow it, and do not follow the divergent ways, for they will take you away from my path,'" [SŪRAH AL-ANʿĀM (6): 153] — that is (a reference to) the lines to the right and left of that straight line."[2]

---

1 — Collected by Al-Harawī in *Dhammul-Kalām* (924) and At-Tabarānī in *Al-Awsat* (7662) it was declared 'hasan' by Shaikh Al-Albānī in his checking of *Al-Mishkāt* then later declared 'weak' by Shaikh Al-Albānī in *Adh-Dhaʿīfah* (1862) and *Dhaʿīful Jāmiʿ* (5877) and this was his final verdict upon it. It is likewise a statement of some of the salaf such as Hasan Al-Basrī (110H) (*Muʿjam Ibnil Aʿrābi*: (4/417) Abū Is-hāq As-Sabīʿī Al-Hamadānī (129H) (Collected by Al-Firyābī in *Al-Qadr* (341)) and Ibrāhīm Ibn Maysarah (132H) (*Dhammul-Kalām*: 928) and Al-Awzāʿī (157H) (*Dhammul-Kalām* : 923) and Fudhail Ibn ʿIyādh (187H) (Collected by Ad-Dīnūri in *Al-Mujālasah wa Jawāhirul ʿIlm* (1/413)

Benefit of the hadīth: The hadīth indicates that honouring an innovator is considered a major sin and is considered aiding the destruction of Islām.

2 — Collected by Ahmad (1/435) and Ad-Dārimī (202) and Muhammad Ibn Nasr Al-Marwazī in *As-Sunnah* (9) and Hākim (2/248) and declared 'hasan-sahīh' by Shaikh Al-Albānī in *At-Taʿlīqātul Hisān* (1/146).

[٢٩] - وَقَالَتْ عَائِشَةُ رَضِيَ اللّٰهُ عَنْهَا وَأَرْضَاهَا - تَلَا رَسُولُ اللّٰهِ «هُوَ الَّذِي

أَنْزَلَ عَلَيْكَ الْكِتَابَ مِنْهُ آيَاتٌ مُحْكَمَاتٌ هُنَّ أُمُّ الْكِتَابِ وَأُخَرُ مُتَشَابِهَاتٌ

فَأَمَّا الَّذِينَ فِي قُلُوبِهِمْ زَيْغٌ فَيَتَّبِعُونَ مَا تَشَابَهَ مِنْهُ ابْتِغَاءَ الْفِتْنَةِ وَابْتِغَاءَ تَأْوِيلِهِ»

{آل عمران: ٧} قَالَت: سَمِعْتُ رَسُولَ اللّٰهِ صَلَّى اللّٰهُ عَلَيْهِ وَسَلَّمَ يَقُول: «إِذَا رَأَيْتُمُ الَّذِينَ

يُجَادِلُونَ فِيهِ فَهُمُ الَّذِينَ عَنَى اللّٰهُ، فَاحْذَرُوهُمْ»

29 — 'Ā'ishah (رَضِيَ اللّٰهُ عَنْهَا) said: "The Messenger of Allāh
(صَلَّى اللّٰهُ عَلَيْهِ وَسَلَّمَ) recited (the statement of Allāh): 'It is He who has sent down to you
(O Muhammad صَلَّى اللّٰهُ عَلَيْهِ وَسَلَّمَ) the book. In it are clear verses — they
are the foundation of the book, and others not entirely clear. So as
for those in whose hearts there is a deviation (from the truth) they
follow that which is not entirely clear thereof seeking fitnah and
seeking for its interpretation...'" [SŪRAH ĀL-IMRĀN (3):7]

She said: "I heard the Messenger of Allāh (صَلَّى اللّٰهُ عَلَيْهِ وَسَلَّمَ) say: 'If you
see those who argue about it then these are the ones Allāh has
intended (with this verse) so be aware of them!'"[1]

•

[٣٠] - وقال (صَلَّى اللّٰهُ عَلَيْهِ وَسَلَّمَ): مَا ضَلَّ قَوْمٌ بَعْدَ هُدًى كَانُوا عَلَيْهِ إِلاَّ أُوتُوا الْجِدَالَ

ثُمَّ قَرَأَ {مَا ضَرَبُوهُ لَكَ إِلاَّ جَدَلاً بَلْ هُمْ قَوْمٌ خَصِمُونَ}.

30 — He also said: "No people go astray after once being upon
guidance, except that they take to argumentation," then he recited
(the statement of Allāh) "They did not quote this example to you

---

Benefit of the hadīth: The hadīth indicates an encouragement to cling to the Sunnah and
to abandon the varying paths of innovation.

1 — Collected by Al-Bukhārī (4547) and Muslim (2665)

Benefit of the hadīth: The hadīth indicates that from the traits of the people of deviation
and innovation is their arguing and debating about ambiguous verses in the Qur'ān.

except for argumentation. Nay, but they are a quarrelsome people."[1]
— SŪRAH AZ-ZUKHRUF (43):58

The Virtue of Clinging to the Sunnah During Afflictions

[٣١] - وقال (ﷺ): الْمُتَمَسِّكُ بِسُنَّتِي عِنْدَ فَسَادِ أُمَّتِي لَهُ أَجْرُ خَمْسِينَ
شَهِيدًا.

31 — He (ﷺ) said: "The one who clings to my Sunnah during (times of) fitnah in the Ummah, bears the reward of fifty martyrs."[2]

•

---

1 — Collected by Ahmad (5/256) and At-Tirmidhī (3253) and Ibn Mājah (48) and declared 'hasan' by Shaikh Al-Albānī in *Sahīh At-Targhīb* (141).

Benefit of the hadīth: The hadīth indicates a warning against argumentation in the religion, and that it is the way of the people of misguidance.

2 — Collected by Ibn Battah in *Al-Ibānatul Kubrā* (1/344) with a weak chain of narration. Al-Baihaqī in *Zuhdul-Kabīr* (207) and Ibn Bushrān (2/31) with the wording "...*one hundred martyrs.*" (Declared 'very weak' by Al-Albānī in *Adh-Dha'īfah* (326). There also occurs in the *Al-Mu'jamul-Awsat* of At-Tabarānī the wording "...*he has the reward of a martyr*" and it is declared 'weak' by Shaikh Al-Albānī in *Dha'īful Jāmi'* (5913).

There does occurs in *Al-Mu'jamul-Kabīr* of At-Tabarānī (9/28) a similar hadīth with the wording: "Indeed before you are days of patience. The one who holds onto his religion in those days will receive the reward of fifty martyrs from you." Declared 'sahīh' by Shaikh Al-Albānī in *Sahīhul Jāmi'* (2234), and in another wording: "Indeed before you are days of patience. The one who holds onto his religion in those days will receive the reward of fifty of you." So they said: "Oh Prophet of Allāh (fifty) of them?" He said: "No! Of you!" Collected by Al-Marwazī in *As-Sunnah* (14) and declared 'sahīh' by Shaikh Al-Albānī in *As-Sahīhah* (494). This does not indicate that the one who holds onto the sunnah in the later days is better than the companions of the Prophet, since there is a difference between virtue and reward. The fact one may receive greater reward does not indicate that he is more virtuous.

Benefit of the hadīth: The hadīth indicates the lofty station and reward for clinging to the sunnah during times of affliction.

[٣٢] - وقال (صَلَّى ٱللَّٰهُ عَلَيْهِ وَسَلَّمَ): الْمُتَمَسِّكُ بِدِينِهِ عِنْدَ فَسَادِ النَّاسِ كَالْقَابِضِ عَلَى الْجَمْرِ.

32 — He (صَلَّى ٱللَّٰهُ عَلَيْهِ وَسَلَّمَ) also said: "The one who holds on to his religion when the people are corrupt is like the one who holds on to hot coal."[1]

•

[٣٣] - وقال (صَلَّى ٱللَّٰهُ عَلَيْهِ وَسَلَّمَ): الْمُتَمَسِّكُ بِدِينِهِ فِي الْهَرَجِ كَالْمُهَاجِرِ إِلَيَّ.

33 — He (صَلَّى ٱللَّٰهُ عَلَيْهِ وَسَلَّمَ) also said: "The one who holds onto his religion during periods of bloodshed is like one who makes migration to me."[2]

•

[٣٤] - وقال (صَلَّى ٱللَّٰهُ عَلَيْهِ وَسَلَّمَ) «بَدَأَ الْإِسْلَامُ غَرِيبًا وَسَيَعُودُ كَمَا بَدَأَ غَرِيبًا فَطُوبَى لِلْغُرَبَاءِ». قَالُوا يَا رَسُولَ اللهِ مَنِ الْغُرَبَاءُ قَالَ: «الَّذِينَ إِذَا فَسَدَ النَّاسُ صَلَحُوا»

34 — He (صَلَّى ٱللَّٰهُ عَلَيْهِ وَسَلَّمَ) also said: "Islām began as something strange and it will return to being something strange so give glad tidings

---

1 — The hadīth occurs a version with slightly different wording in the *Sunan* of At-Tirmidhī (2260): "There will come upon the people a time wherein remaining patient upon ones religion will be like holding onto hot coal." Declared 'sahīh' by Shaikh Al-Albānī in *Sahīh Sunan At-Tirmidhī* (2260). There also occurs in the wording: "For one to hold onto my sunnah when my Ummah differs will be like holding onto hot coal." Declared 'hasan' by Shaikh Al-Albānī in *Sahīhul Jāmi'* (6676)

Benefit of the hadīth: The hadīth indicates the difficulty of clinging to the Sunnah during times of affliction. It likewise indicates the evil effect of afflictions upon peoples practice of the religion.

2 — In Sahīh Muslim (2948) there occurs the wording: *"Worship during periods of bloodshed is like unto making migration to me."*

Benefit of the hadīth: The hadīth indicates the difficulty of clinging to the religion during times of affliction and bloodshed and the immense reward for the one who does so.

to the strangers." They said: "Oh Messenger of Allāh; and who are the strangers?" He said: "Those who rectify themselves when the people become corrupt."[1]

The Command of the Prophet (ﷺ) Concerning his Companions, and the Prohibition Against Speaking Ill Regarding Any of Them.

[٣٥] - وقال (ﷺ): اللَّهَ اللَّهَ فِي أَصْحَابِي لاَ تَتَّخِذُوهُم غَرَضًا بَعْدِي؛ فَمَنْ أَحَبَّهُم فَبِحُبِّي أَحَبَّهُم، وَمَنْ أَبْغَضَهُمْ فَبِبُغْضِي أَبْغَضَهُم، وَمَنْ آذَاهُم فَقَدْ آذَانِي، وَمَنْ آذَانِي فَقَدْ آذَى اللَّهَ، وَمَنْ آذَى اللَّهَ يُوشِكُ أَنْ يَأْخُذَه.

35 — He (ﷺ) also said: "Be mindful of Allāh! Be mindful of Allāh in relation to my companions! Do not make them a target after me (i.e. after my death). Thus, whosoever loves them, does so based on his love for me, and whosoever hates them, he does so based upon his hatred for me. Whoever harms them, harms me and whoever harms me, harms Allāh and whoever harms Allāh then he is soon to take him (with His wrath)."[2]

•

[٣٦] - وقال (ﷺ): لاَ تَسُبُّوا أَصْحَابِي فَوَالَّذِي نَفْسِي بِيَدِهِ لَوْ أَنْفَقَ أَحَدُكُمْ مِثْلَ أُحُدٍ ذَهَبًا مَا بَلَغَ مُدَّ أَحَدِهِمْ وَلا نَصِيفَهُ.

---

1 — Collected by Ibn Battah in Al-Ibānatul Kubrā (2/490) and Ad-Dūlabi in Al-Kunā (2/595) and Ad-Dāni in As-Sunan Al-Wāridah fil Fitan (3/633) — declared 'sahīh' by Shaikh Al-Albānī in As-Sahīhah (1273).

Benefit of the hadīth: The hadīth indicates the fact that the religion will become strange in the later days, due to the people's widespread departure from the true Sunnah of the Prophet in that time as mentioned by Imam Ibnil-Qayyim.

2 — Collected by At-Tirmidhī (3862) and Khallāl in As-Sunnah (3/513) and declared 'weak' in Dha'īful Jāmi' (1160).

Benefit of the hadīth: The fact that hatred for the companions of the Messenger indicates hatred of the Messenger himself. In it is a warning against disparaging them in any way.

36 — He (صَلَّىٱللَّهُعَلَيْهِوَسَلَّمَ) also said: "Do not curse my companions, for by Him in whose hand is my soul, if one of you were to give as charity the likes of Mount Uhud in gold, it would not equate to the handful of charity one of them has given, nor half of it (i.e. a handful)."[1]

•

[٣٧] - وَقَالَ مُعَاذٌ قَالَ لِي النَّبِيُّ (صَلَّىٱللَّهُعَلَيْهِوَسَلَّمَ): يَا مُعَاذُ أَطِعْ كُلَّ أَمِيرٍ وَصَلِّ

خَلْفَ كُلِّ إِمَامٍ وَلاَ تَسُبَّنَّ أَحَدًا مِنْ أَصْحَابِي.

37 — Mu'ādh said: "The Prophet (صَلَّىٱللَّهُعَلَيْهِوَسَلَّمَ) said to me: 'Oh Mu'ādh! Obey every amīr (ruler), and pray behind every Imām, and do not curse any of my companions.'"[2]

•

[٣٨] - وَوَضَعَ رَسُولُ اللَّهِ (صَلَّىٱللَّهُعَلَيْهِوَسَلَّمَ) يَدَهُ عَلَى لِحْيَةِ عُمَرَ بنِ الخَطَّابِ -

رَضِيَ اللَّهُ عَنْهُ - ثُمَّ قَالَ: «يَا عُمَرُ إِنَّا لِلَّهِ وَإِنَّا إِلَيْهِ رَاجِعُونَ» قَالَ عُمَرُ: قُلْتُ

نَعَم بِأَبِي وَأُمِّي يَا رَسُولَ اللَّهِ: إِنَا لِلَّهِ وَإِنَّا إِلَيْهِ رَاجِعُونَ، فَمَا ذَاكَ؟ قَالَ: «إِنَّ

---

1 — Collected by Al-Bukhārī (3470) and Muslim (6651) Abī 'Āsim in *As-Sunnah*: (2/478).

Benefit of the hadīth: The hadīth indicates the great virtue of the companions and the fact that no one after them can equal them even if they perform the same deeds as them or greater.

2 — Collected by Ibn 'Adiyy in *Al-Kāmil* (2/80) and At-Tabarānī in *Al-Kabīr* (20/173) and declared 'weak' by Shaikh Al-Albānī in *Adh-Dha'ifah* (2795).

Benefit of the hadīth: The hadīth indicates the command to obey the Muslim leader, and the prohibition against cursing the Companions of the Prophet. It also indicates that the origin is the permissibility of praying behind the imām that is known as '*mastūr*' (an individual we do not know about) until it becomes clear that he is upon an innovation that is considered disbelief. The scholars mention a principle and that is: whosoever's prayer is sound for himself (meaning that he is not upon an innovation that is considered kufr), then the prayer is sound if he leads other than himself. It is not a condition that we probe the Imām concerning his belief, but if it becomes clear to us that he is upon a belief that is considered kufr, the prayer is abandoned behind him.

جِبْرِيلَ أَتَانِي آنِفًا فَقَالَ: يَا مُحَمَّدُ إِنَّا لِلَّهِ وَإِنَّا إِلَيْهِ رَاجِعُونَ إِنَّ أُمَّتَكَ مَفْتُونَةٌ

بَعْدَكَ بِقَلِيلٍ غَيْرِ كَثِيرٍ. قُلْتُ: يَا جِبْرِيلُ أَفِتْنَةُ ضَلَالٍ أَمْ فِتْنَةُ كُفْرٍ؟ قَالَ: كُلٌّ

سَيَكُونُ. قُلْتُ: كَيْفَ يَضِلُّونَ أَوْ يَكْفُرُونَ وَأَنَا مُخَلِّفٌ بَيْنَ أَظْهُرِهِمْ كِتَابَ اللهِ.

قَالَ: بِكِتَابِ اللَّهِ يَضِلُّونَ يَتَأَوَّلُهُ كُلُّ قَوْمٍ عَلَى مَا يَهْوُونَ فَيَضِلُّونَ بِهِ.»

38 — The Messenger of Allāh (ﷺ) [on an occasion] held
the beard of 'Umar Ibn Al-Khaṭṭāb (ﷺ) and said: "From Allāh
we have come and to Allāh we will return." 'Umar said: "So I said:
'Yes! May my mother and father be ransomed for you! From Allāh we have
come and to Allāh we will return! But what is the matter?'"

He said: "Indeed Jibrīl came to me earlier and said: 'Oh Muhammad!
From Allāh we have come and to Allāh we will return! Indeed your Ummah
will be put to trial not long after you.' So I said: 'Oh Jibrīl will it be the
trial of misguidance or the trial of disbelief?' He said: 'All of that will occur.'
So I said: 'How will they be misguided or disbelieve, when I am leaving the
book of Allāh with them?' He said: 'It is with the book of Allāh that they
will be misguided, each people will interpret it according to their desires and
they will go astray on that basis.'"[1]

•

[٣٩] - وَقَالَ الْحَسَنُ: قَالَ النَّبِيُّ (ﷺ): «مَثَلُ أَصْحَابِي مَثَلُ الْمِلْحِ فِي

الطَّعَامِ» ثُمَّ قَالَ «هَيْهَاتَ ذَهَبَ مِلْحُ الْقَوْمِ»

---

1 — Collected by Al-Fasawī in Al-Ma'rifah (2/308); his version mentions that 'Umar
said: "The Messenger of Allāh held my beard and I could see grief in his face and he
said: 'Indeed Jibrā'īl came to me earlier and said...'" — until the end of the hadīth, and it
was collected by Ibn Abī 'Āsim in As-Sunnah (311) and declared 'very weak' by Shaikh
Al-Albānī in Ad-Dha'īfah (5498) due to the presence of Maslamah Ibn 'Alī Al-Khushani
who is declared 'abandoned' as occurs in At-Taqrīb.

Benefit of the hadīth: The hadīth indicates the fact that trials and afflictions will come
to this Ummah beginning shortly after the death of the Prophet. It also shows that the
main cause of misguidance, will be individuals misinterpreting the Book of Allāh based
upon desires.

39 — Al-Hasan said: "The Prophet (صَلَّى اللهُ عَلَيهِ وَسَلَّمَ) said: "The example of my companions is as the example of salt in food." Then he (Hasan) said: "Alas! The people have lost their salt!"[1]

•

[٤٠] - وَدَخَلَ (صَلَّى اللهُ عَلَيهِ وَسَلَّمَ) المَسْجِدَ وَمَعَهُ أَبُو بَكَرٍ عَنْ يَمِينِهِ وَعُمَرُ عَنْ يَسَارِهِ فَقَالَ: هَكَذَا نُبْعَثُ يَوْمَ الْقِيَامَةِ وَهَكَذَا نَدْخُلُ الجَنَّةَ.

40 — He (صَلَّى اللهُ عَلَيهِ وَسَلَّمَ) entered the masjid and he had Abū Bakr to his right and 'Umar to his left then he said: "This is how we will be raised on the Day of Judgement and this is how we will enter Jannah."[2]

•

---

1 — Collected by Abdur-Razzāq in *Al-Musannaf* (20377) and 'Abdullāh Ibn Mubārak in *Az-Zuhd* (572) Ahmad in *Fadhā'ilus-Sahābah* (17, 173) and declared *'very weak'* by Shaikh Al-Albānī in *Adh-Dha'īfah* (1762). Imāmul-Bukhārī collects (3589) upon the authority of Ibn 'Abbās the sermon of the Messenger wherein he said: "For indeed people will become abundant but the *ansār* will become small in number, to the extent that they will become like salt in food." Thus the narration has an origin and Allāh knows best. Al-'Aini mentions in his explanation of *Sahīh Al-Bukhārī; 'Umdatul Qāri* (16/155): "The angle of resemblance here is (only) that of a small amount rectifying the food and not the angle of abundant salt corrupting food." (i.e. It should not be said that too much of that which has come from the companions is harmful.)

Benefit of the narration: The narration indicates the status of the companions of the Prophet and the deficiency that will occur within the Ummah due to their absence. It also indicates the importance of returning to their understanding in affairs of the dīn.

2 — Collected by At-Tirmidhī (3669) and Ahmad in *Fadhā'ilus-Sahābah* (1/106) and declared *'weak'* by Shaikh Al-Albānī in *Al-Mishkāt* (6054).

Benefit of the hadīth: The hadīth indicates the noble station of the two companions, Abū Bakr and 'Umar and that the Prophet will enter Jannah with them on both sides of him. It also indicates the abhorrent nature of cursing Abū Bakr and 'Umar — (رَضِيَ اللهُ عَنْهُمَا) — to the extent that Imam Ahmad held that whosoever curses them disbelieves, even if he does not curse the rest of his companions.

[٤١] - وقال (ﷺ): مَا مِنْ نَبِيٍّ إِلَّا لَهُ وَزِيرَانِ مِنْ أَهْلِ السَّمَاءِ وَوَزِيرَانِ

مِنْ أَهْلِ الْأَرْضِ، فَأَمَّا وَزِيرَايَ مِنْ أَهْلِ السَّمَاءِ فَجِبْرِيلُ وَمِيكَائِيلُ، وَأَمَّا وَزِيرَايَ

مِنْ أَهْلِ الْأَرْضِ فَأَبُو بَكْرٍ وَعُمَرُ رَضِيَ اللَّهُ عَنْهُمَا.

41 — He – (ﷺ) also said: "There is no Prophet except that he has two ministers from the inhabitants of the heavens and two ministers from the inhabitants of the world. As for my two ministers from the inhabitants of the sky, then they are Jibrīl and Mīkā'īl. As for my ministers from the inhabitants of the earth, then they are Abū Bakr and 'Umar."[1]

•

[٤٢] - وقال (ﷺ): لَا تَسْتَقِرَّ مَحَبَّةُ الْأَرْبَعَةِ إِلَّا فِي قَلْبِ مُؤْمِنٍ تَقِيٍّ أَبِي

بَكْرٍ وَعُمَرَ وَعُثْمَانَ وَعَلِيٍّ رَضِيَ اللهُ عَنْهم.

42 — He (ﷺ) also said: "The love of these four, does not reside except in the heart of the believer that fears Allāh: Abū Bakr and 'Umar and 'Uthmān and 'Alī."[2]

•

---

1 — Collected by Al-Bukhārī in At-Tārīkhul Kabīr (1/159) and At-Tirmidhī (3680) and others and declared 'weak' by Shaikh Al-Albānī in Dha'īful-Jāmi' (5223).

Benefit of the hadīth: The hadīth indicates that Abū Bakr and 'Umar are considered the two ministers of the Prophet — (ﷺ).

2 — Collected by 'Abd Ibn Humaid (1464) and Ahmad in Al-War' (p.81) and in Fadhā'ilus-Sahābah (1/427) In its chain is the weak narrator Yazīd Ibn Hibbān An-Nabati and its chain is also broken. Hāfidh Ibn Hajr mentioned in Al-Matālibul-'Āliyah' (16/276) "This (chain of transmission) is disconnected."

Benefit of the hadīth: The hadīth indicates that love for the four caliphs of the Prophet (ﷺ) is from Īmān.

[٤٣] - وقال (صَلَّى ٱللَّهُ عَلَيْهِ وَسَلَّمَ): أَنَّ اللَّهَ افْتَرَضَ عَلَيْكُم حُبَّ أَبِي بَكرٍ وَعُمَرَ وَعُثْمَانَ وَعَلِيٍّ رَضِيَ اللَّهُ عَنْهُم كَمَا افْتَرَضَ عَلَيكم الصَّلَاةَ وَالصِّيَامَ وَالْحَجَّ فَمَنْ أَبْغَضَ وَاحِدًا مِنْهُم أَدْخَلَهُ اللَّهُ النَّارَ.

43 — He (صَلَّى ٱللَّهُ عَلَيْهِ وَسَلَّمَ) also said: "Indeed, Allāh has made it compulsory upon you to love Abū Bakr, 'Umar, 'Uthmān and 'Alī. Just as He has made compulsory upon you to perform the Salāh, Siyām and Hajj. Whosoever hates one of them then Allāh will enter them into the fire."[1]

•

[٤٤] - وقال (صَلَّى ٱللَّهُ عَلَيْهِ وَسَلَّمَ): مَنْ سَبَّ أَصْحَابِي فَعَلَيْهِ لَعْنَةُ اللهِ وَلَعْنَةُ اللَّاعِنِينَ وَالْمَلَائِكَةِ وَالنَّاسِ أَجْمَعِينَ.

44 — He (صَلَّى ٱللَّهُ عَلَيْهِ وَسَلَّمَ) also said: "Whoever curses my Companions, then upon him is the curse of Allāh, the curse of those who curse, the curse of the angels and the curse of all of the people."[2]

•

[٤٥] - وَقَالَ (صَلَّى ٱللَّهُ عَلَيْهِ وَسَلَّمَ): لَا تَسُبُّوا أَصْحَابِي فَإِنَّهُ يَجِيءُ قَوْمٌ فِي آخِرِ الزَّمَانِ يَسُبُّونَ أَصْحَابِي فَلَا تُصَلُّوا عَلَيْهِم وَلَا تُصَلُّوا مَعَهُم وَلَا تُنَاكِحُوهم وَلَا تُجَالِسُوهُم وَإِنْ مَرِضُوا فَلَا تَعُودُوهُم.

---

1 — It is mentioned by As-Suyūṭī in *Al-Jāmi'ul-Kabīr* and Imām Adh-Dhahabī mentioned in *Al-Wāhiyāt* and says "In it is 'Umar Ibn Ibrāhīm Al-Kurdi who is a fabricator of hadīth." It is also collected by Ibn 'Asākir in his *Tārīkh* (39/127) — in its chain of narration is Ahmad Ibn Nasr Ad-Dhāri'i; Imām Dāraqutni referred to him as a dajjāl!

Benefit of the hadīth: The hadīth indicates that hatred for the four caliphs of the Prophet causes the curse of Allāh to fall upon an individual.

2 — Collected by At-Ṭabarānī and declared 'sahīh' by Shaikh Al-Albānī in *As-Sahīhah* (2340).

45 — He (ﷺ) also said: "Do not curse my Companions! For indeed there will come towards the end of time, a people who will curse my companions. So do not pray upon them, do not pray with them, do not marry them and do not sit with them. If they are sick, then do not visit them."[1]

•

[٤٦] - وَقَالَ ابْنُ عَبَّاسَ لَا تَسُبُّوا أَصْحَابَ مُحَمَّدٍ - (ﷺ) - فإِنَّ اللَّهَ قَدْ أَمَرَنَا بِالِاسْتِغْفَارِ لَهُمْ وَهُوَ يعلم أَنَّهُمْ سيقتلون

46 — Ibn 'Abbās (68H) (رضي الله عنهما) said: "Do not curse the companions of Muhammad (ﷺ). For indeed Allāh commanded us to seek forgiveness for them, and He knew that they would dispute (with each other)."[2]

---

1 — Collected by Al-Khallāl in As-Sunnah (769) and Al-Khatīb in Al-Kifāyah (p.103). It was mentioned by Al-Hindi in Kanzul-Umāl (11/542) and he mentions: "Adh-Dhahabī said: "It is 'munkar jiddan'" (i.e. very weak narration in which a weak narrator opposes the narration of the trustworthy scholars of hadīth).

Benefit of the hadīth: The hadīth indicates that the Prophet foretold the appearance of the Rāfidhah. It similarly indicates the fact they are not to be sat with, prayed with, prayed upon, married, or visited.

2 — Collected by Ahmad in Fadhā'ilus-Sahābah (16) and Al-Ājjuri in Ash-Sharī'ah (1908) and Al-Lillakā'ī (7/1318) in its chain is an unnamed narrator. The narration was collected by Ahmad Ibn Mani' as mentioned by Hāfidh Ibn Hajr in Al-Matālib Al-'Āliyah (17/74) and Al-Busairī in It-hāf Al-Khīratul-Mahirah (7/388) who mentioned: "In it is an unnamed narrator." Shaikhul-Islām mentions the narration in Minhājus-Sunnah (2/22) and instead of رجل (a man) he mentions رجاء (who could possibly have been Rajā Ibn Haiwa; a trustworthy narrator who was from the Tābi'īn and would normally occur in the place it is presumed he is in. If it were so, the chain would be authentic, as Shaikhul-Islām mentioned). Though by gathering its various chains it becomes clear that those who have reported the chain narrate it as 'a man' and not Rajā (therefore a manuscript error) which gives strength to those who hold the chain is broken and Allāh knows best.

Benefit of the narration: The narration indicates that the Salaf understood one is to seek forgiveness for the companions and mention them honourably. One of the main reasons innovated sects speak ill of them is due to the dispute that occurred after the death of the Messenger. Here Ibn 'Abbās indicates the justification some use to speak ill of them is illegitimate.

Statements of the Khulafā Ar-Rāshidūn Regarding Clinging to the Sunnah

[٤٧] - وَقَالَـت عَائِشَـةُ رَضِـيَ اللَّهُ عَنْهَـا أُمِـرُوا بِالاسـتِغْفَارِ لِأَصْحَـابِ مُحمـدٍ فَسَـبُّوهم.

47 — ʾĀʾishah (58H) (رَضِيَٱللَّهُعَنْهَا) said: "They were commanded to seek forgiveness for the companions of Muhammad (صَلَّىٱللَّهُعَلَيْهِوَسَلَّمَ) — and they (turned around and) cursed them."[1]

•

[٤٨] - وَقَالَ أَبُو بَكرٍ الصِّدِّيقُ (رَضِيَٱللَّهُعَنْهُ) أَيُّ سَمَاءٍ تُظِلُّنِي وَأَيُّ أَرْضٍ تُقِلُّنِي إِذَا قُلْتُ فِي كِتَابِ اللَّهِ مَا لَا أَعْلَمُ.

48 — Abū Bakr As-Siddīq (13H) (رَضِيَٱللَّهُعَنْهُ) said: "Which sky shall shelter me, and which earth shall hold me, if I were to say about the book of Allāh what I do not know!"[2]

The Sunnah is the Rope of Allāh

[٤٩] - وَقَالَ أَبُو بَكرٍ الصِّدِّيقُ (رَضِيَٱللَّهُعَنْهُ) السُّنَّةُ حَبْلُ اللَّهِ الْمَتِينُ فَمَن تَرَكَهَا فَقَـد قَطَعَ حَبْلَهُ مِنَ اللَّهِ.

---

1 — Collected by Muslim (3022). Benefit of the narration: The narration indicates the fact that the Rāfidhah who curse the companions have contradicted the commands present within the texts to mention them with good and seek forgiveness for them.

2 — Collected by At-Tabarī (1/35) and by Ibn ʿAbdil-Barr in *Jāmiʿu Bayānil-ʿIlm* (2/833/1561). In a variant wording: *"...if I were to speak about the book of Allāh with my opinion!"* Collected by Al-Baihaqī in *Ash-Shuʿab* 3/540 and Hāfidh Ibn Hajr declared its chain disconnected in *Al-Fat-h* (13/336-337).

Benefit of the narration: The narration indicates the Salaf found it abhorrent to speak about the book of Allāh based upon opinions or desires. The narration with this wording is not present from Abū Bakr, but there is a popular narration with the wording: *"I will not leave anything the Messenger used to do except that I perform it. For indeed I fear that If I leave something from his affair that I will go astray."* Collected by Al-Bukhārī (3093).

49 — Abū Bakr As-Siddīq (13H) (رَضِيَاللهُعَنْهُ) said: "The Sunnah is the firm rope of Allāh, whosoever abandons it, then he has severed his rope from Allāh."[1]

•

[٥٠] - وَقَالَ عُمَرُ بْنِ اَلْخَطَّابِ (رَضِيَاللهُعَنْهُ) أَصْحَابُ الرَّأْيِ أَعْدَاءُ السُّنَنِ، أَعْيَتْهُمُ الْأَحَادِيثُ أَنْ يَحْفَظُوهَا وَتَفَلَّتَتْ مِنْهُمْ فَلَمْ يَعُوهَا فَقَالُوا بِالرَّأْيِ فَضَلُّوا وَأَضَلُّوا.

50 — 'Umar Ibnil-Khattāb (32H) (رَضِيَاللهُعَنْهُ) said: "The people of opinion are the enemies of the Sunan! They became fatigued with memorising hadīth, thus it (i.e. Hadīth) escaped them, and they did not understand them, so they began to speak with opinion, thus they went astray and lead others astray."[2]

•

[٥١] - وقَالَ عُمَرُ (رَضِيَاللهُعَنْهُ) الْقُرْآنُ كَلاَمُ اللَّهِ - عَزَّ وَجَلَّ - فَلَا تُحَرِّفُوهُ إِلَى غَيْرِهِ.

---

1 — The narration with this wording is not present from Abū Bakr, but there is a popular narration with the wording: "I will not leave anything the Messenger used to do except that I perform it. For indeed I fear that If I leave something from his affair that I will go astray." Collected by Al-Bukhārī (3093).

Benefit of the narration: The narration indicates that the salaf understood, that the command to cling to the rope of Allāh in SUURAH ĀLI-'IMRĀN, is a command to hold onto the Sunnah.

2 — Collected by Ad-Dāraqutnī in *As-Sunan* (4280) and Al-Lillakā'ī (201) and Al-Harawī in *Dhammul-Kalām* (259) with variant wording and declared 'sahīh' by Imām Ibnul-Qayyim in *Al-I'lām* (1/64) and Shaikh Al-Albānī in *An-Nasīhah* (199).

Benefit of the narration: The narration indicates that one should be cautious of the people of opinion, and that the reason they began to speak with opinion is due to the fact that memorising and studying the Sunnah exhausted them. They consequently began to rely upon opinion, and went astray and misguided others in the process. Thus the constant study of the Sunnah, is a striking characteristic of the people of Sunnah.

51 — 'Umar (32H) (رَضِيَ ٱللَّهُ عَنْهُ) said: "The Qur'ān is the speech of Allāh, so do not distort it and thereby change it (through false interpretation) to something else!"[1]

•

[٥٢] - وَقَالَ عُمَرُ (رَضِيَ ٱللَّهُ عَنْهُ) أَنَّ اللَّهَ - عَزَّ وَجَلَّ - لَم يَأْمُرْ عِبَادَهُ إِلَّا بِمَا يَنْفَعُهُم

وَلَم يَنْهَهُم إِلَّا عَمَّا يَضُرُّهُم

52 — 'Umar (32H) (رَضِيَ ٱللَّهُ عَنْهُ) said: "Indeed Allāh (عَزَّوَجَلَّ) has not commanded his worshippers except with that which will benefit them, and He has not prohibited them except from that which is harmful to them."[2]

---

1 — Collected by Ad-Dārimī (3358) and 'Abdullāh Ibn Ahmad in *As-Sunnah* (1/144-145) and Al-Ājjurī in *Ash-Sharī'ah* (156) with the wording: *"The Qur'ān is the speech of Allāh so do not deviate its meanings with your opinions"* — in its chain of narration is Laith Ibn Abī Sulaim who is weak.

Benefit of the narration: The narration indicates that distorting the book of Allāh is not only by changing its wording but it is primarily done through its mis-interpretation even if the actual word are not altered. Distortion of the text occurs in two ways: [1] DISTORTION OF WORDING, and [2] DISTORTION OF MEANING. This was the manner in which the previous scriptures were initially distorted.

2 — Shaikhul-Islām attributes the statement to Qatādah in *Majmū' Al-Fatāwā'* (1/217): "Indeed Allāh did not command His servants with that which He commanded them with, due to any need that He has for them. Neither did He prohibit them from that which He prohibited them from, due to miserliness. Rather He commanded them with that which is beneficial to them and He prohibited them from what was harmful to them."

Benefit of the narration: The narration indicates that all prohibitions and commands in the religion returns back to this principle. That is: Allāh has not commanded His worshippers except with that which will benefit them, and He has not prohibited them except from that which is harmful to them. The textual origin of the statement occurs in the statement of Allāh — The Most High: *"Verily, Allāh enjoins justice and Al-Ihsan (Excelling in excellence) and giving aid to kith and kin and He prohibits lewdness, evil deeds and transgression, He admonishes you, that you may take heed!"* [Sūrah An-Nahl (16): 90]. So, whether one is acquainted with the specific wisdoms related to a particular command or prohibition or not, this is a broad general principle with all commands and prohibitions.

The Blameworthy Nature of Following Desires

$$[٥٣] - وَقَالَ عُثْمَانُ (رَضِيَاللَّهُعَنْهُ) الْبَاطِلُ فِيمَا وَافَقَ النَّفْسَ وَإِن رَأَيْتَ أَنَّ لِلَّهِ - عز وجل - فِيهِ طَاعَةُ.$$

53 — 'Uthmān (35H) — (رَضِيَاللَّهُعَنْهُ) said: "Falsehood is in that which agrees with one's inner desires, even if you feel that obedience to Allāh is manifest in that manner."

•

$$[٥٤] - وَقَالَ عَلِيٌّ (رَضِيَاللَّهُعَنْهُ) الْهَوَى يَصُدُّ عَنِ الْحَقِّ.$$

54 — 'Alī (40H) — (رَضِيَاللَّهُعَنْهُ) said: "(Following) Desires (is a factor) that prevents people from the truth."[1]

•

$$[٥٥] - وَقَالَ عَلِيٌّ كَرَّمَ اللَّهُ وَجْهَهُ: الْهَوَى عِنْدَ مَن خَالَفَ السُّنَةَ حَقٌّ وَإِنْ ضُرِبَتْ فِيهِ عُنُقُهُ.$$

55 — 'Alī (40H) — May Allāh ennoble his face[2] — said: "(The following of) Desires is truth, to the one who opposes the sunnah, even if his neck is severed due to it."

•

---

1 — Collected by Ibnul-Mubārak in *Az-Zuhd* (255) and Ibn Abī Shaibah in *Al-Musannaf* (34495) and in its chain is an unknown narrator.

Benefit of the narration: The narration indicates that desires prevents an individual from seeing the truth and following it.

2 — Specifying 'Alī with special du'ā is as Imām Ibnil-Qayyim mentions: *"Making something specific without a specifier"* — see *Jalā'ul-Afhām* (p.259). It should be noted though that in many of the earlier books of the Salaf, these special supplications were added by the manuscript scribes and were not mentioned by the author himself, as is detected when one compares various manuscripts of one book.

Benefit of the narration: The narration indicates that when desires overcomes the heart, the person of desires is willing to die for his falsehood.

[٥٦] - وَقَالَ ابنُ عَبَّاسٍ (رَضِيَ الله عَنْهُمَا) لَا تَضْرِبُوا كِتَابَ اللهِ بَعْضَهُ بِبَعْضٍ

56 — Ibn 'Abbās (68H) (رَضِيَ الله عَنْهُمَا) said: "Do not use the book of Allāh against itself (i.e. use some verses as arguments against others)."[1]

•

[٥٧] - وَجَلَدَ عُمَرُ (رَضِيَ الله عَنْهُ) صَبِيغًا التَّمِيمِي فِي مُسَائِلَتِهِ فِي حُرُوفٍ مِن القُرْآن.

57 — 'Umar (32H) (رَضِيَ الله عَنْهُ) had (an individual called) Sabīgh At-Tamīmi whipped due to his provocative questioning concerning certain letters in the Qur'ān.[2]

•

---

1 — Collected by Ibn Abī Shaibah (30794) and Al-Khallāl in *As-Sunnah* (1953) and Al-Harawī in *Dhammul-Kalām* (171) and Al-Qāsim Ibn Salām in *Fadhā'ilul-Qur'ān* (637).

Benefit of the narration: The narration indicates that verses of the book of Allāh are not to be used against other verses. This is because the Qur'ān does not contradict itself, a person with knowledge would be acquainted with this fact. While the person of desires takes some of the verses of the Qur'ān in isolation to others and goes astray due to this. If one is not clear about how to reconcile the verses of the Qur'ān, he should return the affair to someone who knows.

2 — Collected by Ibn Abī Shaibah (11/426) and Ad-Dārimī (146) and Ibn Wadhāh In *Al-Bid'ah'* (159) Ibn Kathīr mentions in *Musnad Fārūq* (2/606): "The story of Sabīgh Ibn 'Asl At-Tamīmi with 'Umar Ibn Al-Khattāb is popular and it is as though — and Allāh knows best — he disciplined him (as head of state) when it became clear to him that his questioning was done to cause confusion not to seek clarity or establish a proof, as is done by many of the ignorant people of philosophy or the misguided people of innovation."

Benefit of the narration: The narration indicates that the Salaf understood the heinous nature of innovation, such that those who had authority and jurisdiction would discipline the people of desires due to the harm and confusion they created. In doing so they were acting upon the statement of the Prophet: "*Whoever from you sees an evil then let them change it with their hands.*" Changing evil with ones hands returns back to the dictates of those in positions of authority.

[٥٨] - وَقَالَ ابْنُ مَسْعُودٍ (رَضِيَاللَّهُعَنْهُ) إِذَا سَمِعْتَ اللَّهَ - عَزَّ وَجَلَّ - يَقُولُ كَذَا وَكَذَا فَأَصْغِ لَهَا سَمْعَكَ فَإِنَّمَا هُوَ خَيْرٌ تُؤْمَرُ بِهِ أَوْ شَرٌّ تُنْهَى عَنْهُ.

58 — Ibn Masʿūd (32H) (رَضِيَاللَّهُعَنْهُ) said: "If you hear Allāh — The Mighty and Majestic — say such and such, then give the statement your attention. For indeed it is (either) good you are being commanded with, or evil you are being prohibited from."[1]

•

[٥٩] - وَقَالَ ابْنُ مَسْعُودٍ (رَضِيَاللَّهُعَنْهُ): الْقُرْآنُ كَلاَمُ اللَّهِ - عَزَّ وَجَلَّ - فَمَنْ قَالَ فِيهِ شَيْئًا فَإِنَّمَا يَتَقَوَّلُهُ عَلَى اللَّهِ - عز وجل.

59 — Ibn Masʿūd (32H) (رَضِيَاللَّهُعَنْهُ) said: "The Qurʾān is the speech of Allāh — The Mighty and Majestic — so whosoever says anything concerning it, he is speaking concerning Allāh; The Mighty and Majestic."[2]

•

[٦٠] - وَقَالَ ابْنُ عُمَرَ: مَنْ تَرَكَ السُّنَّةَ كَفَرَ

---

1 — Benefit of the narration: The narration indicates that the correct attitude of the believer is to hear and obey the text of the book and the Sunnah. The believer does not make understanding the wisdom behind the commands and prohibitions a prerequisite to following them. If he understands them that is a bonus, but the believer knows that whatever Allāh commands him with, or prohibits him from, then it is either good he is being called to, or harm he is being prevented from. The people of desires often reject established texts on the basis that they 'do not make sense' (to them!) or that they contradict their desires.

2 — Collected by ʿAbdullāh Ibn Ahmad in *As-Sunnah* (100) with the wording: "The Qurʾan is the speech of Allāh — The Mighty and Majestic — so whosoever rejects any of it then he has rebutted Allāh the Most High."

Benefit of the narration: The narration indicates that the Salaf understood that the Qurʾān is the speech of Allāh, and the speech of Allāh is one of His attributes. Whosoever speaks concerning the Qurʾān then he is speaking about Allāh's speech. Whosoever speaks about Allāh's speech, is speaking about Allāh. Thus, let him exercise extreme caution when doing so!

60 — Ibn 'Umar (73H) said: "Whosoever leaves the Sunnah disbelieves."[1]

•

[٦١] - وَقَالَ عُمَرُ بِنِ عَبْدِ العَزِيزِ: السُّنَّةُ إِنَّمَا سَنَّهَا مَنْ عَلِمَ مَا جَاءَ فِي
خِلاَفِهَا مِنَ الزَّلَلِ وَلَهُم كَانُوا عَلَى المُنَازَعَةِ وَالجَدَلِ أَقْدَرُ مِنْكُم

61 — 'Umar Ibn 'Abdul-'Azīz (141H) said: "The Sunnah was established by one[2] who knew the error and misguidance of that

---

1 — Collected by 'Abdur-Razzāq As-San'ānī in *Al-Musannaf* (4381) and 'Abd Ibn Humaid in *Al-Muntakhab* (820) and Al-Bazzār (5929) with the wording: Upon the Authority of Muwarriq Al-'Ijlī who said: "Ibn 'Umar was asked concerning praying while upon a journey? He said: *'It is performed in sets for two rak'ah and whosoever opposes the Sunnah disbelieves'"* — and in variant wordings: *"Whosoever leaves the Sunnah disbelieves."* Hāfidh Ibn Hajr mentions in *Al-Matālibul-'Āliyah* (736): *"Its chain of transmission is authentic."*

Note: what is intended by the statement of Ibn 'Umar is either that the one who intentionally rejects the Sunnah disbelieves; or that opposing the Sunnah is an act of kufr but the one who does so, doesn't become a disbeliever — depending upon the nature of the opposition.

Benefit of the narration: The narration indicates that the one who intentionally abandons the Sunnah, obstinately rejecting it, disbelieves. His disbelief is considered major kufr that ejects him from the religion. The whole of the religion is based upon the Sunnah. The issues the Sunnah commands us with are of two types: That which is wājib, and that which is desirable. If one abandons the Sunnah unknowingly, or leaves a Sunnah that is desirable, then this does not constitute disbelief or even a sin. If one abandons the compulsory affairs of the Sunnah, but does not make *istihlāl* (i.e. he does not deem it halāl for him to do so), knowing that he is wrong, then this is considered minor disbelief or *kufr 'amali* (disbelief in action). It does not eject a person from the religion, but is considered a major sin. There is a difference of opinion concerning the one who lazily abandons one of the five pillars of Islām, with the exception of the first pillar, the *shahādatain*. Thus, the type of kufr is relative to the nature of the abandonment, we must look at the type of Sunnah he abandoned, and the reason for the abandonment. This statement of Ibn 'Umar, intended to exhort and premonish, is to be understood in this light.

2 — Referring to Allāh or His Messenger. See: *'Aunil-Ma'būd* (12/239).

which opposes it. Indeed they (the pious predecessors) had more ability to argue and debate than we do."[1]

•

[٦٢] - وَقَالَ رَجُلٌ لِابْنِ عَبَّاسٍ (رَضِيَاللَّهُعَنْهَا): الْحَمْدُ لِلَّهِ الَّذِي جَعَلَ هَوَانَا عَلَى هَوَاكُم فَقَالَ ابْنُ عَبَّاسٍ (رَضِيَاللَّهُعَنْهَا)، أَنَّ اللَّهَ لَم يَجعَل فِي هَذِهِ الأَهْوَاءِ شَيئًا مِنَ الخَيرِ وَإِنَّمَا سُمِّيَ هَوَى لِأَنَّهُ يَهْوِى بِصَاحِبِهِ فِي النَارِ

62 — A man said to Ibn ʿAbbās (68H) – (رَضِيَاللَّهُعَنْهَا) "Praise be to Allāh, who has made our desires in accordance with yours!" So Ibn ʿAbbās (68H) – (رَضِيَاللَّهُعَنْهَا) said: "Indeed Allāh has not placed in desires anything from good! It is referred to as desires (hawā) because it 'yahwī' (causes a person to descend falling) into the fire!"[2]

•

---

1 — Collected by Ibn Battah in *Al-Ibānatul-Kubrā* (164) and in *Sunan Abī Dāwūd* (4612) and declared 'sahīh' by Shaikh Al-Albānī in *Sahīh Sunan Abī Dāwūd* (4612) and Al-Ājurrī in *Ash-Sharīʿah* (529: Ad-Damījī print) and Ibn Wadhāh in *Al-Bidʿah* (74: Salīm Print).

Benefit of the narration: The narration indicates that though the Salaf were far more knowledgeable than those who came later, they were not given to debating and arguing with the people of desires concerning the Sunnah, except in necessity. They knew, this opened a door to spreading doubts and misguidance, thus they abandoned it. They understood that the Sunnah was based in Allāh's wisdom and as such was not open for debate. They merely studied it, memorised it, acted upon it, and encouraged others to do the same.

2 — Collected by Ibn Battah in *Al-Ibānatul-Kubrā* (238) and Al-Lillakā'ī (225) though in their versions, Ibn ʿAbbās responded: "All desires are misguidance." Also Al-Ājurrī in *Ash-Sharīʿah* (126) and ʿAbdur-Razzāq in *Al-Musannaf* (20102) and Al-Harawī in *Dhammul-Kalām* (797) from the statement of Imām Shaʿbi without mention of the initial question.

Benefit of the narration: The narration indicates that the Salaf understood that there is no good in following desires, even if they are the desires of the more knowledgeable individuals from the best generation of this ummah. We see Ibn ʿAbbās nurturing his students upon this understanding, and explaining that desires by definition, lead to the fire, when followed independently.

[٦٣] - وَقَالَ الْحَسَنُ ومجاهدٌ وأَبُو الْعَالِيَةِ إِنَّمَا سُمِّيَ هَوًى لِأَنَّهُ يَهْوِي بِصَاحِبِهِ فِي النَّارِ.

63 — Al-Hasan (110H), Mujāhid (104H) and Abul-'Āliyah[1] (93H) all said: "*Hawā* (desires) were named *Hawā* because it '*Yahwī*' (causes a person to descend falling) into the fire!"[2]

•

[٦٤] - وَقَالَ الْحَسَنُ: مَا مِن دَاءٍ أَشَدَّ مِن هَوًى خَالَطَ قَلْباً

64 — Al-Hasan said (110H): "There is no illness that affects the heart worse than *Hawā* (desires)."[3]

•

[٦٥] - وَقَالَ أَبُو قِلَابَة إِيَّاكُمْ وَأَصْحَابَ الْخُصُومَاتِ فَإِنِّي لَا آمَنُ أَن يَغْمِسُوكم فِي ضَلَالَتِهِم، أَوْ يُلَبِّسُوا عَلَيكم مَا تَعْرِفُونَ

65 — Abū Qilābah[4] (276H) said: "Be aware of the (deviated) people of argumentation, for indeed I cannot guarantee security for you, from them immersing you into their misguidance, or causing you to become confused about what you already know."[5]

---

1 — His name is Rufai' Ibn Mihrān Ar-Rayāhi Al-Basri. He saw Abū Bakr and prayed behind 'Umar and was taught the Qur'ān by Ubayy Ibn Ka'b.

2 — Ad-Dārimi in his *Sunan* (409 and 416) and Al-Lillakā'ī (229) and other than him have collected its likes from Imām Ash-Sha'bi

Benefit of the narration: The narration indicates that the Salaf saw desires, the same way they saw disease. They considered desires the worse of the sicknesses of the heart.

3 — Collected by Ahmad in *Az-Zuhd* (p.264) and 'Abdullāh Ibn Ahmad in *As-Sunnah* (1/138).

4 — His name is 'Abdul-Malik Ibn Muhammad Ar-Raqāshī (276H).

5 — Collected by Al-Ājurrī in *Ash-Sharī'ah* (p.59) and Al-Bayhaqī in *Al-I'tiqād* (p.118) and Ad-Dārimī in *As-Sunan* (1/108) and Al-Harawī in *Dhammul-Kalām* (819) and Al-Baghawī in *Sharhus-Sunnah* (1/228) and Al-Lillakā'ī (244) with the wording: كَثِيرًا مِمَّا تَعْرِفُونَ "..*much of what you know*". Ibn Battah mentions the above version in *Al-Kubra* (363 and

[٦٦] - وَكَرِهَ عَطَاءٌ وَطَاوُوسٌ وَمُجَاهِدٌ وَالشَّعْبِيُّ وَإِبْرَاهِيمُ أَنْ يُفْتُوا فِي شَيْءٍ

مِنَ الخُصُومَاتِ، وَقَالُوا: الخُصُومَاتُ مَحْقُ الدِّينِ وَقَالُوا: مَا خَاصَمَ وَرِعٌ قَطُّ.

66 — 'Atā' (114H),[1] Tāwūs (106H),[2] Mujāhid (104H), Ash-Sha'bī
(100H),[3] and Ibrāhīm (Ibn Yazīd An-Nakha'ī: 100H) all disliked
giving verdicts pertaining to argumentation. They all said:
"Argumentation destroys the religion! A person of piety is never
given to argumentation."[4]

•

[٦٧] - وَقَالَ عِمْرَانُ بْنُ الحُصَيْنِ: «الحَيَاءُ مِنَ الإِيمَانِ» فَقَالَ رَجُلٌ عِنْدَهُ:

فِي الحِكْمَةِ مَكْتُوبٌ: إِنَّ مِنَ الحَيَاءِ ضَعْفًا وَمِنْهُ وَقَارًا. فَقَالَ عِمْرَانَ: أُحَدِّثُكَ

عَنْ رَسُولِ اللهِ (ﷺ) وَتُحَدِّثُنِي عَنْ صُحُفِكَ؟! لَا أُكَلِّمُكَ أَبَدًا!

67 — 'Imrān Ibn Husayn (52H) mentioned (the hadīth of the
Messenger of Allāh ﷺ): *"Shyness is from Īmān"* so a man said
in his presence: "It is written in (books of Arab) wisdom, that from

---

369) and also collects two other versions with variant wordings: (364) بَعْضَ مَا تَعْرِفُونَ *"..some
of what you know",* and without the statement وَلَا تُجَادِلُوهُمْ *"..and do not argue with them"* (365)
مَا كُنْتُمْ تَعْرِفُونَ *"..what you used to know".* They are all close in meaning.

Benefit of the narration: The narration indicates that the Salaf understood that nearness
to the people of desires and argumentation is to be feared for more than one reason. [1]
Either they will immerse you into their deviation, or [2] they will cause you to become
confused about what you already know. Both of these are evil outcomes, thus they
warned against them.

1 — He is 'Atā' Ibn Rabāh Al-Makkī (114H)

2 — He is Tāwūs Ibn Kaysān (106H)

3 — He is Āmir Ibn Sharāhīl (100H)

4 — Imām Al-Ājurri collects in *Ash-Shari'ah'* (p.56) the narration of 'Abdul-Karīm Al-
Jazari: *"A person of piety is never given to argumentation."*

Benefit of the narration: The narration indicates that the Salaf disliked argumentation to
the extent they disliked giving verdicts in relation to it. They saw that it was not the way
of the pious.

shyness there is weakness, and from it, there is (what is considered praiseworthy) composure."

So 'Imrān said: "I narrate to you from the Messenger of Allāh (صَلَّى ٱللَّهُ عَلَيْهِ وَسَلَّمَ) and you narrate to me from your scrolls?! I will never speak to you again!"[1]

•

[٦٨] - وذُكِرَ عِنْدَ عِمْرَانَ بْنِ الْحُصَيْنِ الْحَدِيثُ فَقَالَ رَجُلٌ مِنَ الْقَوْمِ: لَوْ قَرَأْتُمْ سُورَةً مِنْ كِتَابِ اللَّهِ كَانَ أَفْضَلَ مِنْ حَدِيثِكُمْ، فَقَالَ عِمْرَانُ: إِنَّكَ لَأَحْمَقُ! أَتَجِدُ الصَّلَاةَ فِي كِتَابِ اللَّهِ مُفَسَّرَةً؟ أَتَجِدُ الزَّكَاةَ فِي كِتَابِ اللَّهِ مُفَسَّرَةً؟ إِنَّ الْقُرْآنَ أَحْكَمَهُ وإِنَّ السُّنَّةَ فَسَّرَتْهُ.

68 — A hadīth was mentioned in the presence of 'Imrān Ibn Husayn (52H). One of the people said: "If only you had recited a verse of the Qur'ān it would have been better than this hadīth of yours!" So 'Imrān said: "Indeed you are a fool! Do you find the prayer

---

1 — Collected by Al-Bukhārī (5766) and Muslim (165) the version in Al-Bukhārī and Muslim but the hadīth mentioned in it is the statement of the Prophet: "Shyness does not come except with good." These versions also mention that the one who made the comment was noble Tābi'i; Bushair Ibn Ka'b Al-'Adawī.

Benefit of the narration: The narration indicates that the Salaf would employ boycotting as a disciplinary method. Corporal punishment is in the hands of the ruler, while boycotting is in the hands of other than the ruler. The narration also indicates that the boycott may be used with issues of opposition to the Sunnah other than innovation. Here we have a case of opposition to the sunnah and not innovation. In other narrations, Ibn 'Umar boycotted his own son for saying about the hadīth: *"Do not prevent the female slaves of Allāh from the mosques of Allāh."* His son said: *"As for me then I will prevent them!"* So, Ibn 'Umar refused to speak to him again until he died. 'Abdullāh Ibn Mughaffal prohibited a relative from flicking pebbles, quoting a hadith to him in that regard. When he proceeded to flick them again, he refused to speak to him for the rest of his life! Ibn 'Umar and Ibn Mughaffal were not in any political position of authority. The boycott is a method of treating obstinance and is also used to protect oneself from harm on occasions. Anyone who claims it is abrogated within the religion must substantiate this claim with evidence. The companions utilised it after the death of the Prophet thus it is known that it has not been abrogated by revelation.

being mentioned in the Qur'ān in detail?! Do you find Zakāh in the Qur'ān mentioned in detail?! Certainly, the Qur'ān makes general mention (of affairs) and certainly, the Sunnah explains it!"[1]

•

[٦٩] - وقال المِقْدَامُ بنُ مَعْدِي كَرِب: حَرَّمَ رَسُولُ اللهِ - (صَلَّى اللَّهُ عَلَيْهِ وَسَلَّمَ) - يَومَ خَيبَرَ أَشْيَاءً فَقَالَ «يُوشِكُ رَجُلٌ عَلَى أَرِيكَتِهِ يَأْتِيهِ مِمَّا أَمَرْتُ أَو نَهَيتُ فَيَقُولُ: دَعُونَا مِنْ هَذَا مَا نَدْرِي مَا هَذَا عَلَيكُم بِكِتَابِ اللهِ فَلَأَعْرِفَنَّ الرَّجُلَ مِنْكُم.»

69 — Al-Miqdām Ibn Ma'dīkarib (91H) said: "The Messenger (صَلَّى اللَّهُ عَلَيْهِ وَسَلَّمَ) made a number of things prohibited on the day of Khayber and he said: 'There is soon to be an individual sitting on his recliner, and there comes to him that which I have commanded or prohibited and he says: *"We are not interested in this! We do not know this! Just cling to the book of Allāh."* I certainly know (that) a man from you (will do so).'"[2]

•

[٧٠] - وَقَالَ رَجُلٌ لِابْنِ عُمَرَ (رَضِيَ اللَّهُ عَنْهُمَا): أَرَأَيْتَ أَرَأَيْتَ. فَقَالَ اجْعَل أَرَأَيْتَ بِالْيَمَنِ إِنَّمَا هِيَ السُّنَنِ.

---

1 — Collected by Ibn Battah in *Al-Ibānatul-Kubrā* (65) Al-Harawī in *Dhammul-Kalām* (244) and Al-Ājjurī in *Ash-Shari'ah* (p.49) with slightly variant wording.

Benefit of the narration: The narration indicates that the Salaf understood that the Qur'ān is not understood in isolation from the Sunnah. The Sunnah explains the Qur'ān and clarifies it. It brings detail to general texts that cannot be understood or practiced without the detail present within the Sunnah.

2 — Collected by Ahmad (4/120) and At-Tirmidhī (2664) and Abū Dāwūd (4606) and Ad-Dārimī (606).

Benefit of the hadīth: The hadīth indicates the Messenger of Allāh prophesied the coming of a sect known as the Qur'āniyyūn. A sect claiming that their only source of the religion is the Qur'ān and that we have no need for the Sunnah. This group appeared in the second century after hijra and from the first of those who rebutted them was Al-Imām Ash-Shāfi'ī. They also re-appeared in the 19th century and individuals continue to carry this false belief up until this very day.

70 — A man said to Ibn 'Umar (رَضِيَ اللهُ عَنْهُمَا): *"Do you not see (such and such) do you not see (such and such)"* (i.e. expressing his opinions) so Ibn 'Umar said, "Leave *'Do you not see...'* in Yemen (i.e. abandon your opinions!). Indeed this affair is the Sunnah! (i.e. it returns back to the Sunnah)."[1]

[٧١] - وَقَالَ الشَّعْبِيُّ: مَا قَضَيْتُ لِي رَأْيًا قَطُّ

71 — Ash-Sha'bi[2] (100H) said: "I have never implemented my opinion ever."[3]

•

[٧٢] - وقَالَ قَتَادَةُ: لَمْ أَفْتِ بِرَأْيِ مُنْذُ ثَلَاثِينَ سَنَة

72 — Qatādah (117H) said: "In thirty years, I have never passed a verdict based upon my own opinion."[4]

---

1 — Collected by Al-Bukhārī (1611) and Ibn Battah in *Al-Ibānatul-Kubrā* (606) and its wording is "Put *'do you not see'* in the sky" (i.e. throw your opinions to the skies).

Benefit of the narration: The narration indicates that which the Salaf were upon from following the text and nurturing their students upon that.

2 — He is 'Āmir Ibn Sharāhīl, Abū 'Amr Al-Kūfī.

3 — Ad-Dārimī collects a narration of A'mash: "I have never heard Ibrāhim (An-Nakha'ī) ever give his (own) opinion." Ibn Sa'd collects the narration of Muhammad Ibn Juhādah in *At-Tabaqātul-Kubrā* (6/250): "'Āmir Ash-Sha'bī was asked about something and he had no answer, so it was said: *'Give your own opinion on it.'* He responded: *'And what will you do with my opinion?! Urinate on my opinion!'*"

4 — *Al-Ja'diyāt* (1058) and Ibn Sa'd in *At-Tabaqātul-Kubrā* (7/229). Imām Adh-Dhahabī mentions in *Siyar* (5/273) the statement of Abū Hilāl who said: "I asked Qatādah about an issue and he said: *'I don't know,'* so I said to him: *'Mention your own opinion.'* He said: *'I haven't spoken (about knowledge) using my own opinion for forty years!'*" He was approximately 50 years old at the time!

Benefit of the narration: The narration indicates that scholars do not give verdicts based upon their own opinion. Even in issues known as the *nawāzil* (those new issues that appear that require an Islamic verdict) they pass rulings based upon the implementation of well-established principles based in the texts. Since no-one receives revelation after the Messenger of Allāh.

[٧٣] - وَقَالَ الْحَسَنُ: شِرَارُ عِبَادِ اللَّهِ الَّذِينَ يَتَّبِعُونَ شِرَارَ الْمَسَائِلِ لِيُعْمُوا بِهَا
عِبَادَ اللهِ

73 — Al-Hasan (110H) said: "The worst of the servants of Allāh are those who follow the worst of issues, seeking to blind the servants of Allāh (from the path of truth) by way of that."[1]

•

[٧٤] - وَقَالَ مَيْمُون بن مِهْرَان فِي قَوْلِهِ - عَزَّ وَجَلَّ - {فَإِنْ تَنَازَعْتُمْ فِي شَيْءٍ
فَرُدُّوهُ إِلَى اللَّهِ وَالرَّسُولِ} قال. الرَّدَّ إِلَى اللَّهِ: إِلَى كِتَابِهِ، وَالرَّدَّ إِلَى الرَّسُولِ -
إِذَا قُبِضَ - إِلَى سُنَّتِهِ.

74 — Maimūn Ibn Mihrān (117H) said concerning the statement of Allāh: 'And if you differ in an issue then return it back to Allāh and His Messenger if you believe in Allāh and the last day,' — he said: "Returning an affair back to Allāh is to return it back to His book and returning back to the Messenger after his death, is to return it back to his Sunnah."[2]

•

[٧٥] - وَقَالَ عِكْرِمَة (فِي قَوْلِهِ تَعَالَى) {أَطِيعُوا اللَّهَ وَأَطِيعُوا الرَّسُولَ وَأُولِي
الْأَمْرِ مِنْكُمْ} قَالَ: أَبُو بَكرٍ وَعُمَرَ رَضِيَ اللهُ عَنْهُمَا.

---

1 — Collected by the author in *Al-Ibānatul-Kubrā* (304) and Ad-Dārimī (106) and Al-Harawī in *Dhammul-Kalām* (529) and Ibn 'Abdil-Barr in *Jāmi'u Bayānil-Ilm Wa-Fadhlihī* (2084) with the wording "...*making things hard upon the servants of Allāh.*"

2 — Collected by the author in *Al-Ibānatul-Kubrā* (58) and At-Tabarī (5/151) and Al-Lillakā'ī (76).

75 — 'Ikrimah (107H)[1] said about the statement of Allāh: *'Obey Allāh and obey the Messenger and those who are in charge of your affairs,'* — he said: "(This refers to) Abū Bakr and 'Umar (رَضِيَ اللهُ عَنْهُمَا)."[2]

The Station of the Sunnah in relation to the Qur'ān[3]

$$[٧٦] - وَقَالَ يَحْيَى بْنِ أَبِي كَثِيرٍ: السُّنَّةُ قَاضِيَةٌ عَلَى الْقُرْآنِ، وَلَيْسَ الْقُرْآنُ بِقَاضٍ عَلَى السُّنَّةِ.$$

76 — Yahyā Ibn Abī Kathīr (132H) said: "The Sunnah has jurisdiction over the book (the Qur'ān), but the book has no jurisdiction over the Sunnah."[4]

•

---

1 — He is 'Ikrimah Ibn 'Abdillāh the freed servant of Ibn 'Abbās.

2 — Collected by the author in *Al-Ibānatul-Kubrā* (57) and At-Tabarī in his *Tafsīr* (5/149) and Ibn Abī Hātim in his *Tafsīr* (5573).

Benefit of the narration: The narration indicates that affairs are to be referred back to the opinions of the companions and that Islamic verdicts after them, are to be judged in accordance with that which they understood.

3 — There is a common error some make in relation to this topic. Often times we hear that: The Sunnah is the second source of legislation in the Sharī'ah. If the intent is that the Qur'ān has a greater station than the Sunnah, in terms of it being the pure speech of Allāh and that all of it is of the highest level of authenticity, then this is correct. But if what is intended by this, is that the Sunnah comes second to the Qur'ān in terms of our relied upon sources of legislation, then this is an error. In relation to legislation, the Qur'ān and the Sunnah work hand in hand, since the Sunnah is the explanation of the Qur'ān as Allāh informs us in the Qur'ān. The Sunnah does not come after the Qur'ān as we hear some mentioning.

4 — Collected by the author in *Al-Ibānatul-Kubrā* (88 and 89) Ad-Dārimi in *As-Sunan* (587) and Al-Harawī in *Dhammul-Kalām* (216). Imām Ahmad said in *Dhammul-Kalām* (213): "I am not bold enough to say that, but the Sunnah explains the Qur'ān and clarifies it."

Benefit of the narration: The narration is a refutation of the Qur'āniyyūn and those who hold their view. The Qur'an requires the Sunnah to clarify it, since Allāh sent the Prophet to explain the Qur'ān. Allāh says: "And we sent to you the reminder that you may explain to them that which was revealed to them."

[٧٧] - وقَالَ حَسَّانَ بنِ عَطِيَّةَ كَانَ جِبرِيلُ عَلَيهِ السَّلَامُ يَنْزِلُ عَلَى النَّبِيِّ (صَلَّىاللهُعَلَيهِوَسَلَّمَ) بِالسُّنَّةِ كَمَا يَنْزِلُ عَلَيهِ بِالْقُرْآنِ يُعَلِّمُهُ إِيَّاهَا كَمَا يُعَلِّمُهُ الْقُرْآنَ.

77 — Hasān Ibn 'Atiyyah (120H) said: "Jibrīl used to descend upon the Messenger of Allāh with the Sunnah just as he would descend upon him with the Qur'ān, teaching it to him as he would teach him the Qur'ān."[1]

•

[٧٨] - وَقَالَ سَعِيدُ بنُ جُبَيرٍ فِي قَوْلِهِ - عَزَّ وجلَّ - {وَعَمِلَ صَالِحًا ثُمَّ اهْتَدَى} قَالَ: «لُزُومِ السُّنَّةِ وَالْجَمَاعَةِ.»

78 — Sa'īd Ibn Jubair (95H) said concerning the statement of Allāh (عَزَّوَجَلَّ): 'And he worked righteous deeds and then was guided' — he said: "He clung to the Sunnah and the Jamā'ah."[2]

•

[٧٩] - حَدَّثَنَا عُبَيدُ اللَّهِ قَالَ لَنَا أَبُو عَلِيٍّ إِسْمَاعِيلُ بْنُ مُحَمَّدٍ الصَّفَّارُ، قَالَ: حَدَّثَنَا أَحْمَدُ بْنُ مَنْصُورٍ الرَّمَادِيُّ، قَالَ: حَدَّثَنَا عَبْدُ الرَّزَّاقِ، عَنْ مَعْمَرٍ، عَنْ قَتَادَةَ، فِي قَوْلِهِ عَزَّ وَجَلَّ: {وَاذْكُرْنَ مَا يُتْلَى فِي بُيُوتِكُنَّ مِنْ آيَاتِ اللَّهِ وَالْحِكْمَةِ} [الأحزاب: ٣٤] قَالَ: «الْقُرْآنُ وَالسُّنَّةُ»

79 — It was narrated to us from 'Ubaidillah (who said that) Abū 'Alī Ismā'īl Ibn Muhammad As-Safār (341H) said: Ahmad Ibn Mansūr

---

1 — Collected by Ad-Dārimī in *As-Sunan* (588).

Benefit of the narration: The narration indicates that the Sunnah was revelation from Allāh just as the Qur'ān is revelation from Allāh, no believer rejects any one of them.

2 — Collected by Al-Asbahānī in *Al-Hujjah Fī Bayānil Mahajjah* (2/405) and Al-Lillakā'ī in *Sharh Usūl I'tiqād Ahlis-Sunnah* (1/71).

Benefit of the narration: The narration indicates that the Salaf understood that true guidance is in to cling to the Book and the Sunnah.

Ar-Ramādi (265H) said to us, 'Abdur-Razzāq (As-San'ānī: 211H) said to us, Ma'mar (154H) said to us upon the authority of Qatādah (117H) who said concerning the statement of Allāh: *'And remember (Oh members of the Prophets family) that which is recited in your houses of the verses of Allāh and the Hikmah,'* [SURATUL AHZĀB (33): 34] — he (Qatādah) said: "The Qur'an and the Sunnah."[1]

•

[٨٠] - قَالَ حَدَّثَنَا أَبُو عَبْدِ اللَّهِ أَحْمَدُ بْنُ عَلِيٍّ بْنُ عَلَاءِ الجَوزَجَانِي قال لنا

عَبْدُ الوَهَّابِ الْوَرَّاقُ - الشَّيخ الصَّالِحِ - قَالَ: حَدَّثَنَا أَبُو مُعَاوِيَةَ، عَنِ الْأَعْمَشِ،

عَنْ مُجَاهِدٍ، قَالَ: «أَفْضَلُ الْعِبَادَةِ حُسْنُ الرَّأْيِ» يَعْنِي السُّنَّةَ

80 — It was narrated to us from Abū 'Abdillāh Ahmad Ibn 'Alī Ibn 'Alā' Al-Jauzajānī who said: "It was narrated to us from 'Abdul-Wahhāb Al-Warrāq — The righteous Shaikh — who said: 'It was narrated to us from Abū Mu'āwiyah, upon the authority of Al-A'mash upon the authority of Mujāhid who said: "The best form of worship is in having sound opinion," meaning the Sunnah.'"[2]

•

---

1 — Collected by Ibn Battah in *Al-Ibānatul-Kubrā* (91 and 218).

Benefit of the narration: The narration indicates the Sunnah is referred to as the "Wisdom" in the Book of Allāh.

2 — Collected by the author in *Al-Ibānatul-Kubrā* (223) and Ibn Abī Shaibah in *Al-Īmān* (p.27).

Benefit of the narration: The narration indicates that opinion in affairs of religion is of two types: [1] Opinion that is based in the Sunnah and/or in the maxims and broad principles indicated by the Sunnah and this is praiseworthy, or [2] Pure opinion and this is blameworthy.

[٨١] - وَقَالَ إِسْحَاقُ بْنُ عِيسَى: سَمِعْتُ مَالِكَ بْنَ أَنَسٍ يَعِيبُ الْجِدَالَ فِي الدِّينِ وَيَقُولُ: «كُلَّمَا جَاءَنَا رَجُلٌ هُوَ أَجْدَلُ مِنْ رَجُلٍ أَرَدْنَا أَنْ نَتْرُكَ مَا جَاءَ بِهِ جِبْرِيلُ إِلَى النَّبِيِّ صَلَّى اللَّهُ عَلَيْهِ وَسَلَّمَ.»

81 — Is-ḥāq Ibn ʿĪsā (214H) said: "I heard Mālik Ibn Anas (dispraising argumentation in the religion saying *Every time there comes to us a man better in argumentation than another, we wish to leave that which Jibrīl brought to the Prophet* ﷺ?!'"[1]

The Blameworthy Nature of Innovation and its People.

[٨٢] - وَقَالَ ابْنُ سِيرِينَ: مَا أَخَذَ رَجُلٌ بِدْعَةً فَرَاجَعَ سُنَّةً.

82 — Ibn Sīrīn (110H) Said: "No man holds onto bidʿah and returns to the Sunnah."[2]

•

[٨٣] - وَقَالَ عَامِرُ بْنُ عَبْدِ اللَّهِ: مَا ابْتَدَعَ رَجُلٌ بِدْعَةً إِلَّا أَتَى غَدًا بِمَا كَانَ يُنْكِرُهُ الْيَوْمَ.

---

1 — Collected by the author in *Al-Ibānatul-Kubrā* (582) and Ahmad in *Al-ʿIlal* (1585) and Al-Lillakāʾī (293).

Benefit of the narration: The narration indicates that the Salaf did not consider someone's opinion correct merely on the basis that he was better in speech and argumentation than another, rather they considered an affair correct due to it agreeing with the Qurʾan and the established Sunnah. It also indicates that the Salaf were averse to argumentation in the affairs of dīn. Their way was to explain and teach the established texts of the Book and the Sunnah.

2 — Collected by Ad-Dārimī (214). Translator's note: The meaning here is that it is a rare occurrence.

Benefit of the narration: The narration indicates that the Salaf observed that once innovation settles in the heart, individuals leaving it and repenting from it is a rarity.

83 — 'Āmir Ibn 'Abdillāh (121H) said: "No man brings about an innovation, except that tomorrow he comes with that which he used to dispraise today."[1]

•

[٨٤] - وَقَالَ ابْنُ عَوْنٍ: إِذَا غَلَبَ ٱلْهَوَى عَلَى ٱلْقَلْبِ اسْتَحْسَنَ ٱلرَّجُلُ مَا كَانَ يَسْتَقْبِحُهُ.

84 — Ibn 'Aun (150H) said: "If desires overpower the heart then a man will begin to deem good that which he used to dispraise."[2]

•

[٨٥] - وَقَالَ ٱلْفُضَيْلِ: لَا يَزَالُ ٱلْعَبْدُ مَسْتُورًا حَتَّى يَرَى قَبِيحَهُ حَسَنًا.

85 — Fudhail[3] (187H) said: "A servant does not cease being noble and inconspicuous, until he considers good that which he (once) deemed despicable."[4]

•

---

1 — The author collects in *Al-Kubrā* (574) the narration of Ibrāhīm An-Nakha'ī: "They (the Salaf) used to hate inconsistency in religion."

2 — 'Abdur-Razzāq (20454) collects upon the authority of Hudhaifah (رَضِيَ ٱللَّهُ عَنْهُ) who said: "Indeed misguidance, true misguidance, is that you deem good that which you used to despise, and that you despise that which you used to deem good, and be aware of inconsistency in religion, for indeed the religion of Allāh is one."

3 — He is Fudhail Ibn 'Iyādh Ibn Mas'ūd At-Tamīmī (187H).

4 — i.e. When he opposes the Sunnah, and his opinions changes due to that, his affair becomes apparent to the people.

Benefit of the narrations: The narrations indicate that the Salaf held that when innovations enter the heart, they cause individuals to diametrically oppose the Sunnah they were previously upon, or to easily deviate from one innovation to another. It also indicates that the yardstick of nobility as far as they were concerned revolved around a person's steadfastness upon the Sunnah.

[٨٦] - وَقَالَ أَبُو الْعَالِيَة: آيَتَانِ فِي كِتَابِ اللَّهِ مَا أَشَدُّهُمَا عَلَى الَّذِينَ يُجَادِلُونَ
غِي الْقُرْآن: {مَا يُجَادِلُ فِي آيَاتِ اللَّهِ إِلَّا الَّذِينَ كَفَرُوا} [غافر: ١٧٦] {وإِنَّ
الَّذِينَ اخْتَلَفُوا فِي الكِتَابِ لَفِي شِقَاقٍ بَعِيدٍ} [البقرة: ١٧٦]

86 — Abul-'Āliyah said: "There are two verses in the book of Allāh
that are very heavy upon those who argue with the Qur'ān: *'No one
argues concerning the verses of Allāh except those who disbelieve'* [SŪRAH
AL-GHĀFIR (40):4] and *'Indeed those who have differed over the book are
in distant splitting.'"* [SŪRAH AL-BAQARAH (2):176].[1]

•

[٨٧] - وَقَالَ أَرْطَأَةُ بْنُ الْمُنْذِرِ: لَأَنْ يَكُونَ ابْنِي فَاسِقًا مِنْ الْفُسَّاقِ أَحَبُّ إِلَيَّ
مِنْ أَنْ يَكُونَ صَاحِبَ الْهَوَى.

87 — Arta'ah Ibnul-Mundhir (163H) said: "That my son be an
open sinner, is more beloved to me than for him to be a person of
desires."[2]

•

[٨٨] - وَقَالَ أَبُو إِسْحَاق الْفَزَارِيُّ: لَأَنْ أَجْلِسَ إِلَى النَّصَارَى فِي بِيَعِهِمْ أَحَبُّ
إِلَيَّ مِنْ الْجُلُوسِ فِي حَلْقَةٍ يَتَخَاصَمُ فِيهَا النَّاسُ فِي دِينِهِمْ.

---

1 — Collected by the author in *Al-Ibānatul-Kubrā* (540, 541) and Al-Harawī in
Dhammul-Kalām (192).

Benefit of the narration: The narration indicates that the Salaf held that the people
of innovation were well known for two characteristics dispraised by the Qur'an. [1]
Blameworthy debate and argumentation about the Qur'an. [2] Dividing and splitting in
their religion.

2 — Collected by Al-Harawī in *Dhammul-Kalām* (929).

Benefit of the narration: The narrations indicates that the Salaf deemed sinning, even
doing so publicly, was less grave than innovation. This is because innovation (even the
type that does not reach the level of disbelief and shirk) is more severe than major sin.

88 — Abū Is-ḥāq Al-Fazārī (185H)[1] said: "That I should sit with Christians in their church, is more beloved to me than to sit in a circle wherein people dispute concerning their religion."[2]

•

[٨٩] - وَقَالَ سَعِيدُ بْنُ جُبَيْرٍ: لَأَنْ يَصْحَبَ ابْنِي فَاسِقًا شَاطِرًا سُنِّيًّا أَحَبُّ إِلَيَّ
مِنْ أَنْ يَصْحَبَ عَابِدًا مُبْتَدِعًا.

89 — Saʿīd Ibn Jubair said: "That my son should accompany a shrewd sinful scoundrel who is Sunnī, is more beloved to me than that he should accompany a devout worshipping innovator."[3]

•

[٩٠] - وَقِيلَ لِمَالِكِ بْنِ مِغْوَلٍ: رَأَيْنَا ابْنَكَ يَلْعَبُ بِالطُّيُورِ فَقَالَ: «حَبَّذَا إِنْ
شَغَلَتْهُ عَنْ صُحْبَةِ مُبْتَدِعٍ.

---

1 — He is Ibrāhīm Ibn Muhammad Ibnil-Hārith Al-Fazārī.

2 — Benefit of the narration: The narrations indicates that the Salaf would prefer to sit in a gathering of Christians than to sit in a gathering of the people of innovation, this is due to the fact that though the first (i.e. sitting in a church) is considered a sin, they knew it would not cause confusion in the heart. While sitting in a gathering of the people of innovation, listening to them misinterpret the verses of the Qur'an, and misconstruing the Sunnah, using the language of Islām, is far more harmful to the heart of the believer. Thus, even though the belief of the Christian is more severe, in that it is shirk, the Salaf would grade danger based upon the effect the gathering would have upon the heart of the believer. On that basis, they would consider a gathering of the people of innovation (even if the innovation did not reach the level of shirk or kufr) more dangerous and harmful to the believer, than a gathering of Christians, which is unlikely to affect change in even the very ignorant Muslim.

3 — Ibn Wadhāh collects a similar narration upon the authority of Al-'Awām Ibn Hawshab.

90 — It was said to Mālik Ibn Mighwal (195H): "We saw your son playing with birds." So he responded, "If it busies him from accompanying a person of innovation, then I commend it!"[1]

•

[٩١] - وَقَالَ ابْنُ شَوْذَبٍ: مِنْ نِعْمَةِ اللَّهِ عَلَى الشَّابِّ وَالْأَعْجَمِيِّ إِذَا تَنَسَّكًا أَنْ يُوَفَّقَا لِصَاحِبِ سُنَّةٍ يَحْمِلُهُمَا عَلَيْهَا لِأَنَّ الشَّابَّ وَالْأَعْجَمِيَّ يَأْخُذُ فِيهِمَا مَا سَبَقَ إِلَيْهِمَا.

91 — Ibn Shawdhab[2] said (156 or 157H): "From the blessings of Allāh upon a youth and upon a non-Arab when they become religious, is that Allāh grants them success to accompany a person of Sunnah who carries them[3] upon it. For indeed the young one and the Non-Arab are both taken by the first to approach them."[4]

•

[٩٢] - وَقَالَ عَمْرُو بْنُ قَيْسٍ الْمُلَائِيُّ: إِذَا رَأَيْتَ اَلشَّابَّ أَوَّلَ مَا يَنْشَأُ مَعَ أَهْلِ اَلسُّنَّةِ وَالْجَمَاعَةِ فَارْجُهُ وَإِذَا رَأَيْتَهُ مَعَ أَهْلِ اَلْبِدَعِ فَايَأْسْ مِنْهُ فَإِنَّ اَلشَّابَّ عَلَى أَوَّلِ نُشُوئِهِ.

92 — 'Amr Ibn Qais Al-Mulā'ī (after 140H) said: "If you see a youth starting out with the people of Sunnah and the Jamā'ah, then have hope for him. And if you see him with the people of

---

1 — Benefit of the narrations: The narrations indicates that the Salaf would prefer their children to accompany sinners or to involve themselves in what was considered timewasting, but remain upon the Sunnah, than for them to accompany the people of innovation who would deviate them from the true path of Allāh and His Messenger. This was not that they deemed accompanying sinners or wasting time a minor affair, but that they saw innovations as far worse.

2 — He is 'Abdullāh Ibn Shawdhab Al-Khurasānī (Abū 'Abdur-Rahmān).

3 — i.e. Aids them in understanding it and acting upon it.

4 — Collected by Al-Lillakā'ī (1/60) and Al-Ibānatul-Kubrā (43).

innovation then give up on him, for indeed a youth remains upon the way of those who first nurture him."[1]

•

[٩٣] - وَقَالَ عَمْرُو بْنُ قَيْسٍ: إِنَّ الشَّابَّ لَيَنْشَأُ فَإِنْ آثَرَ أَنْ يُجَالِسَ أَهْلَ العِلْمِ كَادَ يَسْلَمُ وَإِنْ مَالَ إِلَى غَيْرِهِمْ كَادَ يَعْطَبُ.

93 — 'Amr Ibn Qais said: "Indeed a young one sets out and if he prefers to sit with people of knowledge, he is on the verge of salvation. But if he inclines towards other than them then he is on the verge of destruction!"[2]

•

[٩٤] - وَقَالَ حَمَّادُ بْنُ زَيْدٍ: قَالَ لِي يُونُسُ إِنِّي يَا حَمَّادُ إِنِّي لَأَرَى الشَّابَّ عَلَى كُلِّ حَالَةٍ مُنْكَرَةٍ فَلَا أُيِّسُ مِنْ خَيْرِهِ حَتَّى أَرَاهُ يُصَاحِبُ صَاحِبَ بِدْعَةٍ فَعِنْدَهَا أَعْلَمُ أَنَّهُ قَدْ عَطِبَ.

94 — Hammād Ibn Zaid (179H) said: "Yūnus (Ibn 'Ubaid) (139H) said to me: 'Oh Hammād! Indeed, I may see a youth upon various states and forms of evil and I do not give up hope in good coming from him, until I see him accompanying a person of innovation, it is then that I know he is destroyed!'"[3]

•

---

1 — *Al-Ibānatul-Kubrā* (44) and Ibnil-Banā in *Ar-Radd 'alal-Mubtadi'ah* (48).

2 — *Al-Ibānatul-Kubrā* (45).

3 — *Ar-Radd 'alal-Mubtadi'ah* (48)

Benefit of the narrations: The narrations indicate that the youth or non-Arab (who doesn't understand the language of the texts) are vulnerable individuals affected by their first nurture. If they are nurtured by the people of innovation and this settles in their hearts then they would consider this to be something likely to affect them the rest of their lives unless Allāh saves them and guides them.

[٩٥] - وَقَالَ اَلْحَسَنُ: مَا اِزْدَادَ صَاحِبُ بِدْعَةٍ عِبَادَةً إِلَّا اِزْدَادَ مِنَ اللَّهِ بُعْدًا.

95 — Al-Hasan said: "A person of innovation does not increase in worship, except that he increases in distance from Allāh."[1]

•

[٩٦] - وَقَالَ اِبْنُ عَوْنٍ: اَلْمُجْتَهِدُ فِي اَلْعِبَادَةِ مَعَ اَلْهَوَى يَتَّصِلُ جُهْدُهُ بِعَذَابِ اَلْآخِرَةِ.

96 — Ibn 'Aun said: "The one who strives upon performing acts of worship while remaining upon desires, then his striving is connected to the punishment of the Hereafter."

•

[٩٧] - وَقَالَ اَلْأَوْزَاعِيُّ قَالَ إِبْلِيسُ لِأَوْلِيَائِهِ: مِنْ أَيْنَ تَأْتُونَ بَنِي آدَمَ؟ فَقَالُوا: مِنْ كُلِّ بَابٍ قَالَ فَهَلْ تَأْتُونَهُمْ مِنْ قِبَلِ الِاسْتِغْفَارِ؟، قَالُوا إِنَّ ذَلِكَ شَيْءٌ لَا نُطِيقُهُ إِنَّهُمْ لَمُقِرُّونَ بِالتَّوْحِيدِ، قَالَ لَآتِيَنَّهُمْ مِنْ بَابٍ لَا يَسْتَغْفِرُونَ اَللَّهَ مِنْهُ، قَالَ «فَبَثَّ فِيهِمْ اَلْأَهْوَاءَ وَالْبِدَعَ.»

97 — Al-Auzā'ī[2] (157H) said: "Iblīs says to his allies: *'How will you approach the son of Ādam?'* So they said: *'From every door!'* He said: *'But can you approach them from the direction of Istighfār?'*[3] They said: *'Indeed that is something we are not able to do, since they attest to the oneness of Allāh!'* He said: *'I shall approach them from a door for which they will not seek forgiveness from Allāh!'* So he spread among them desires and innovations."

---

1 — *Dhammul-Kalām* of Al-Harawī (477) and Ibn Wadhāh in *Al-Bid'ah* (66).

2 — He is 'Abdur-Rahmān Ibn 'Amr Ibn Abī 'Amr Al-Auzā'ī.

3 — i.e. from the direction of them seeking forgiveness.

The Dispraise for the People of Innovation

[٩٨] - قَالَ سَعِيدُ بْنُ عَنْبَسَةَ: مَا ابْتَدَعَ رَجُلٌ بِدْعَةً إِلَّا غَلَّ صَدْرُهُ عَلَى
المُسْلِمِينَ وَاخْتَلَجَتْ مِنْهُ الأَمَانَةُ.

98 — Saʿīd Ibn ʿAnbasa said: "No person brings about an innovation,
except that his heart is filled with malice for the believers and
amānah (trustworthiness) is stripped from him."[1]

•

[٩٩] - وَقَالَ الأَوْزَاعِيُّ: مَا ابْتَدَعَ رَجُلٌ بِدْعَةً إِلَّا سُلِبَ وَرَعَهُ.

99 — Al-Auzāʿī (157H) said: "No person innovates except that
piety is removed from him."[2]

•

[١٠٠] - وَقَالَ الحَسَنُ: مَا ابْتَدَعَ رَجُلٌ بِدْعَةً إِلَّا تَبَرَّأَ الإِيمَانُ مِنْهُ.

100 — Al-Hasan said: "No person innovates except that Īmān frees
itself from him."

•

[١٠١] - قَالَ ابْنُ عَوْنٍ: مَا ابْتَدَعَ رَجُلٌ بِدْعَةً إِلَّا أَخَذَ اللَّهُ مِنْهُ الحَيَاءَ وَرَكَّبَ
فِيهِ الجَفَاءَ.

101 — Ibn ʿAun said: "No person innovates except that Allāh
removes shame from him, and places negligence within him."[3]

---

1 — Collected by Al-Harawī in Dhammul-Kalām (919) and Al-Hujjah Fī Bayānil-
Mahajjah (1/330).

2 — Collected by Al-Harawī in Dhammul-Kalām (919).

3 — Benefit of the narrations: The narrations indicate that the Salaf knew that
innovations have numerous evil effects upon its proponents. From those evil effects: [1]
Malice and rancour entering their hearts for the believers. [2] Piety is removed from

[١٠٢] - وَقَالَ عُثْمَانُ بْنُ حَاضِرٍ الْأَزْدِيُّ دَخَلْتُ عَلَى ابْنِ عَبَّاسٍ فَقُلْتُ أَوْصِنِي فَقَالَ: عَلَيْكَ بِالِاسْتِقَامَةِ اتَّبِعْ وَلَا تَبْتَدِعْ.

102 — 'Uthmān Ibn Hādhir Al-Azdī said: "I entered upon Ibn 'Abbās (68H) – (رَضِيَاللّٰهُعَنْهُمَا) and said: 'Advise me!' He said: 'Remain upon uprightness, follow (i.e. the Sunnah) and do not innovate!'"[1]

•

[١٠٣] - وَقَالَ ابْنُ مَسْعُودٍ (رَضِيَاللّٰهُعَنْهُ): (اتَّبِعُوا وَلَا تَبْتَدِعُوا فَقَدْ كُفِيتُمْ فَإِنَّ كُلَّ مُحْدَثَةٍ بِدْعَةٌ وَكُلَّ بِدْعَةٍ ضَلَالَةٌ.

103 — Ibn Mas'ūd (رَضِيَاللّٰهُعَنْهُ) said: "Follow! And do not innovate for indeed you have been sufficed. Certainly, every newly invented affair is an innovation and every innovation is misguidance."[2]

•

[١٠٤] - وَقَالَ طَلْحَةُ بْنُ مُصَرِّفٍ: لَا تُحَدِّثْ بِكُلِّ مَا سَمِعْتَ إِلَّا أَنْ يَكُونَ الَّذِي حَدَّثْتُمْ عَلَى السُّنَّةِ.

104 — Talhah Ibn Musarrif (112H) said: "Do not narrate everything you hear — unless the one who narrated to you is upon the Sunnah!"

•

---

them. [3] Shame is removed from them. [4] Negligence is placed within them. [5] Iman is depleted from their hearts, and my possibly disappear. These are just some of the evil effects of innovation upon the heart and thus the Salaf warned staunchly against it fearing these things for the people.

1 — Collected by Al-Harawī in *Dhammul-Kalām* (334) and Ibn Battah in *Al-Ibānatul-Kubrā* (157).

2 — *Al-Ibānatul-Kubrā* (185).

[١٠٥] - وَقَالَ أَبُو إِدْرِيسَ الخَوْلَانِيُّ: لَأَنْ أَرَى فِي المَسْجِدِ نَارًا تَضْطَرِمُ أَحَبُّ إِلَيَّ مِنْ أَنْ أَرَى فِيهِ بِدْعَةً لَا تُغَيَّرُ.

105 — Abū Idrīs Al-Khawlāni[1] (80H) said: "That I should see a fiercely blazing fire in the masjid is more beloved to me than for me to see innovations within it, not being changed."[2]

•

[١٠٦] - وَقَالَ عَطَاءٌ: مَا يَكَادُ اَللَّهُ يَأْذَنُ لِصَاحِبِ بِدْعَةٍ بِتَوْبَةٍ.

106 — 'Atā' said: "Allāh almost never permits a person of innovation to repent."[3]

•

[١٠٧] - وَقَالَ ابْنُ عَبَّاسٍ: مَنْ أَقَرَّ بِاسْمٍ مِنْ هَذِهِ الْأَسْمَاءِ المُحْدَثَةِ فَقَدْ خَلَعَ رِبْقَةَ اَلْإِسْلَامِ مِنْ عُنُقِهِ.

107 — Ibn 'Abbās said: "Whoever attests to, and agrees with, one of these newly invented titles, then he has removed the yoke of Islām from his neck."[4]

---

1 — He is 'Ā'idh Ibn 'Abdillāh Ad-Damishqī.

2 — Benefits of the narration: the narration indicates that the Salaf saw that an innovation being spread or acted upon in the masjid was more painful to them than seeing the masjid on fire. We therefore should pay more concern to ensuring the masjid and its attendees remain upon the Sunnah than we do to making sure the masjid looks clean and beautiful.

3 — Collected in Al-Hilyah (5/198) and Al-Harawī in Dhammul-Kalām (780 and 942) and Al-Lillakā'ī (283).

Benefit of the narration: The narration indicate that the people of innovation rarely repent from their innovations since they see that what they are doing or believing in is good.

4 — Collected by Al-Harawī in Dhammul-Kalām (720) and Ibn Battah in Al-Ibānatul-Kubrā (245).

[١٠٨] - وَقَالَ مَيْمُونُ بْنُ مِهْرَانَ: إِيَّاكُمْ وَكُلَّ اسْمٍ يُسَمَّى بِغَيْرِ الْإِسْلَامِ.

108 — Maimūn Ibn Mihrān said: "Be cautious of any title that is used other than Islām (i.e. other than that indicated by Islām)."[1]

•

[١٠٩] - وَقَالَ مَالِكُ بْنُ أَنَسٍ: لَمْ يَكُنْ مِنْ هَذِهِ الْأَهْوَاءِ عَلَى عَهْدِ النَّبِيِّ (صَلَّىٰ اللَّهُ عَلَيْهِ وَسَلَّمَ) وَلَا أَبِي بَكْرٍ وَلَا عُمَرَ وَلَا عُثْمَانَ.

109 — Mālik Ibn Anas said: "Nothing from these desires were present during the era of the Prophet (صَلَّىٰ اللَّهُ عَلَيْهِ وَسَلَّمَ) nor (during the era of) Abū Bakr, nor 'Umar, nor 'Uthmān."[2]

•

[١١٠] - وَقَالَ مَالِكُ بْنُ مِغْوَلٍ: إِذَا تَسَمَّى الرَّجُلُ بِغَيْرِ الْإِسْلَامِ وَالسُّنَّةِ فَأَلْحِقْهُ بِأَيِّ دِينٍ شِئْتَ.

110 — Mālik Ibn Mighwal said: "If a man refers to himself using other than the titles of Islām and the Sunnah, then attribute him to any religion you wish!"

•

[١١١] - وَقَالَ عَطَاءٌ: إِنَّ فِيمَا أَنْزَلَ اللَّهُ تَبَارَكَ وَتَعَالَى عَلَى مُوسَى عَلَيْهِ السَّلَامُ لَا تُجَالِسْ أَهْلَ الْأَهْوَاءِ فَيُحْدِثُوا فِي قَلْبِكَ مَا لَمْ يَكُنْ.

Benefit of the narration: The narration indicates that the one who attest to an innovation of Kufr or Shirk and finds no issue with it and doesn't detest it with his heart, then his being pleased with Kufr is itself Kufr. This strong statement of Ibn 'Abbās applies to those innovations that are Kufr or Shirk in nature. The innovations of a lesser level must still be detested since they all revolve around changing the true religion that Allāh sent to His Messenger (صَلَّىٰ اللَّهُ عَلَيْهِ وَسَلَّمَ).

1 — Collected by Ibn Battah In *Al-Ibānatul-Kubrā* (211, 235, 236) and Abū Nu'aym in *Al-Hilyah* (4/92).

2 — Collected by Al-Firyābī in *Al-Qadr* (387) and Al-Harawī in *Dhammul-Kalām* (865).

111 — 'Ata' said: "Indeed from that which Allāh revealed to Mūsā, is that *'One should not sit with the people of desires, thus enabling them to introduce to your heart what was not (previously) present (within it)!'*"[1]

•

[١١٢] - وَقَالَ أَبُو قِلَابَةَ: مَا ابْتَدَعَ قَوْمٌ بِدْعَةً إِلَّا اسْتَحَلُّوا فِيهَا السَّيْفَ.

112 — Abū Qilābah said: "No people bring about innovations except that they deem the use of the sword (i.e. against their brothers) permissible."[2]

•

[١١٣] - وَقَالَ أَبُو قِلَابَةَ فِي قَوْلِهِ تَعَالَى: {إِنَّ الَّذِينَ اتَّخَذُوا الْعِجْلَ سَيَنَالُهُمْ غَضَبٌ مِنْ رَبِّهِمْ وَذِلَّةٌ فِي الْحَيَاةِ الدُّنْيَا وَكَذَلِكَ نَجْزِي الْمُفْتَرِينَ} وَقَالَ أَبُو قِلَابَةَ: «فَهِيَ جَزَاءُ كُلِّ مُفْتَرٍ إِلَى يَوْمِ الْقِيَامَةِ.»

113 — Abū Qilābah said about the verse of Allāh: *'Indeed those who took the calf (for worship), wrath from their Lord and humiliation will come upon them in the life of this world. Thus, do We recompense those who invent lies.'* [SŪRAH AL-A'RĀF (7):152] — Abū Qilābah said: "Hence, this is the recompense for anyone that fabricates lies until the day of judgement."[3]

---

1 — Collected by Ibn Battah in *Al-Ibānatul-Kubrā* (362) and Al-Harawī in *Dhammul-Kalām* (781).

2 — Collected by Ad-Dārimī in *As-Sunan* (100) and Al-Firyābī in *Al-Qadr* (368).

Benefit of the narration: The narration indicates that the nature of innovation is such that it often causes its proponents to become physically violent with those who oppose them. This is a reality observed up until the present day.

3 — Collected by At-Tabarī in *At-Tafsīr* (9/70) and Al-Lillakā'ī (288).

Benefit of the narration: The narration indicates that the Sunnah of Allāh with the people of falsehood and innovation, is that they receive a portion of the wrath and humiliation mentioned here in the Quranic verse. If their innovation is considered Shirk,

[١١٤] ـ وَقَالَ أَبُو قِلَابَةَ: «إِنَّ أَهْلَ الْأَهْوَاءِ أَهْلُ ضَلَالَةٍ وَلَا أَرَى مَصِيرَهُمْ إِلَّا إِلَى النَّارِ فَجَرِّبْهُمْ فَلَيْسَ أَحَدٌ مِنْهُمْ يَنْتَحِلُ رَأْيًا أَوْ قَالَ قَوْلاً فَيَتَنَاهَى دُونَ السَّيْفِ وَإِنَّ النِّفَاقَ كَانَ ضُرُوبًا.» ثُمَّ تَلَا: {وَمِنْهُمْ مَنْ عَاهَدَ اَللَّهَ}

114 — Abū Qilābah said: "Indeed the people of desires are people of misguidance! I do not see their final destination except the fire! Test them! Indeed, none of them holds an opinion — or he said: (holds) a position — except that it leads him to the sword! And certainly, hypocrisy is of various types!"

Then he recited the statement of Allāh *"And from them (i.e. The Hypocrites) are those who made a covenant with Allāh..."* — SŪRAH AT-TAWBAH (9): 75[1]

•

[١١٥] ـ وَقَالَ ابْنُ عَبَّاسٍ: مَنْ فَارَقَ الْجَمَاعَةَ شِبْرًا فَقَدْ خَلَعَ رِبْقَةَ الْإِسْلَامِ مِنْ عُنُقِهِ.

115 — Ibn 'Abbās said: "Whosoever splits away from Islām a handspan, then he has certainly taken the yoke of Islām from his neck."[2]

•

---

then their similitude is the same as the Children of Israel who committed Shirk at the time of Mūsā, and indeed we seek refuge in Allāh from this.

1 — Collected by Ad-Dārimī in *As-Sunan* (101) and Al-Firyābī in *Al-Qadr* (376).

2 — This narration is likewise authentically attributed to the Messenger (ﷺ) from his statements. It is collected by Ahmad (5/180) and Abū Dāwūd (4758) and declared 'sahīh' by Shaikh Al-Albānī in *Sahīh Abū Dāwūd* (4758). The same statement has been attributed to 'Alī (﵁) — (see narration 142).

Benefit of the narration: The narration indicates that splitting from the Jamā'ah is a major sin. This strong statement refers to the grave nature of the act and that the one who falls into it is in severe danger as far as his religion is concerned.

[١١٦] - وَقَالَ مُحَمَّدُ بْنُ ٱلْحَنَفِيَّةِ: لَا تَقُومُ ٱلسَّاعَةُ حَتَّى تَكُونَ خُصُومَةُ ٱلنَّاسِ فِي رَبِّهِمْ.

116 — Muhammad Ibnil-Hanafiyyah[1] (died after 80H) said: "The hour will not be established until the argumentation of the people will be about their Lord!"[2]

•

[١١٧] - وَقَالَ عَبْدُ ٱللَّهِ بْنُ عَمْرٍو: يُوشِكُ أَنْ تَظْهَرَ شَيَاطِينُ مِمَّا أَوْثَقَ سُلَيْمَانُ بْنُ دَاوُدَ عَلَيْهِ ٱلسَّلَامُ يُفَقِّهُونَ ٱلنَّاسَ.

117 — 'Abdullāh Ibn 'Amr said: "Shayātīn, from those who were bound and fettered by Sulaimān, the son of Dawūd (عَلَيْهِٱلسَّلَامُ) are upon the verge of appearing (in the guise of individuals) teaching people!"[3]

•

---

1 — He is Muhammad Ibn 'Alī Ibn Abī Tālib, Abul-Qāsim Ibn Al-Hanafiyyah. He was the son of 'Alī Ibn Abī Tālib born of his slave girl, and he is popularly known by his attribution to her.

2 — Collected by Ibn Battah in *Al-Ibānatul-Kubrā'* (616 and 617) and Al-Lillakā'ī (213) and Al-Harawī in *Dhammul-Kalām* (604) with the wording: *"The world will not diminish…"* Prior to this (602) he mentions the statement as a hadīth of the Messenger (صَلَّىٱللَّهُعَلَيْهِوَسَلَّمَ) narrated upon the authority of Abū Hurairah, but in its chain of narration is Abū Qilābah Ar-Ruqāshī, whose name is Abdul-Malik Ibn Muhammad and he is weak. Thus, Imām 'Alī Ibn Al-Madīnī declared this hadīth an erroneous narration, the attribution of which should be to Ibnul-Hanafiyah as his statement: *Dhammul-Kalām* (603).

Benefit of the narration: The narration (and the one that follows it) indicates the foresight of the Salaf, and the fact that their statements, more often than not, are derived from the Sunnah in a general or a specific manner.

3 — Collected by Muslim in the introduction of *Sahīh Muslim* (8) and 'Abdur-Razzāq As-San'ānī in *Al-Musannaf* (20807) and Ad-Dārimī in *As-Sunan* (428).

Benefit of the narration: The narration indicates that the Salaf understood that the newly invented innovations are from the inspiration of devils who either create them, or revamp innovations of old and inspire humans with them.

[١١٨] - وَقَالَ أَيُّوبُ السَّخْتِيَانِيُّ: قَالَ لِي أَبُو قِلَابَةَ عَنِّي أَرْبَعًا: لَا تَقُلْ فِي الْقُرْآنِ بِرَأْيِكَ وَإِيَّاكَ وَالْقَدَرَ وَإِذَا ذُكِرَ أَصْحَابُ رَسُولِ اللَّهِ - صلى الله عليه وسلم - فَأَمْسِكْ وَلَا تُمَكِّنْ أَصْحَابَ الْأَهْوَاءِ مِنْ سَمْعِكَ فَيُنْفِذُوا فِيهِ مَا شَاءُوا.

118 — Ayyūb As-Sikhtiyānī[1] (131H) said: "Abū Qilābah said to me: "Oh Ayyūb! Memorise four things from me:

- Do not speak about the Qur'ān with your opinion,

- Stay away from delving into the affair of Qadr (Devine decree)

- If the companions of the Messenger are mentioned, then refrain

- And do not allow the people of desires to get to your hearing and thus cast into it what they will!"[2]

•

[١١٩] - وَقَالَ إِبْرَاهِيمُ النَّخَعِيُّ فِي قَوْلِهِ - عَزَّ وَجَلَّ - {وَأَلْقَيْنَا بَيْنَهُمُ الْعَدَاوَةَ وَالْبَغْضَاءَ} قَالَ: «هُمْ أَصْحَابُ الْأَهْوَاءِ.»

119 — Ibrāhīm An-Nakha'ī said concerning the statement of Allāh: 'And we placed between them enmity and hatred,' [SŪRAH AL-MĀ'IDAH: 64] — he said: "They are the people of desires."[3]

---

1 — He is Ayyūb Ibn Abī Tamīmah Kaysān As-Sikhtiyānī, Abū Bakr Al-Basrī.

2 — Collected by Ibn Battah in *Al-Ibānatul-Kubrā* (397) and Al-Harawī in *Dhammul-Kalām* (818) and Al-Lillakā'ī (236).

Benefit of the narration: The narration indicates the strong position of the Salaf in relation to these four things. [1] Speaking about the Qur'ān using opinion, [2] Speaking about Qadr (Devine decree) without knowledge, [3] Speaking about the Sahabah except with good, [4] Lending an ear to the people of desires and innovation.

3 — Collected by At-Tabarī in his *Tafsīr* (6/158-159) and Al-Harawī in *Dhammul-Kalām* (820), concerning the statement of Allāh in regard to the Christians ("*So we placed amongst them enmity and hatred until the day of judgement."* — SŪRAH AL-MĀ'IDAH: 14) — he said: "I do not see this enmity and hatred being placed among anyone in this Ummah except the people of divisive desires and hatred."

[١٢٠] - وَقَالَ مُعَاوِيَةُ بْنُ قُرَّةَ: الْخُصُومَاتُ فِي الدِّينِ تَمْحَقُ الْأَعْمَالَ.

120 — Mu'āwiyah Ibn Qurrah[1] (113H) said: "Argumentation in the religion removes blessings from the actions."[2]

•

[١٢١] - وَقَالَ يُوسُفُ بْنُ أَسْبَاطٍ: النَّظَرُ إِلَى صَاحِبِ بِدْعَةٍ يُطْفِئُ نُورَ الْحَقِّ مِنْ الْقَلْبِ.

121 — Yūsuf Ibn Asbāt[3] said: "Looking at a person of bid'ah extinguishes the light of the truth from the heart."[4]

•

Benefit of the narration: The narration indicates that this great Imām and student of 'Abdullāh Ibn Mas'ūd, understood that though the verse was revealed concerning the Children of Israel, the generality of the verse encompassed the people of innovation from this Ummah. Due to their resemblance and similarity in numerous ways to the children of Israel who Allāh dispraised in many places in the Qur'ān.

1 — He is Mu'āwiyah Ibn Qurrah Ibn Iyās Ibn Hilāl Al-Muzanī

2 — Collected by Al-Ājurrī in Ash-Shari'ah (64) and Ibn Battah in Al-Ibānatul-Kubrā (564) and Al-Lillakā'ī (221).

Benefit of the narration: The narration indicates that argumentation in the affairs of religion, strips the blessings of one's dīn and from one's actions. This is due to what it brings about of hate, enmity and doubt.

3 — He is Yūsuf Ibn Asbāt Ash-Shaybānī.

4 — The meaning of this narration is attributed to a number of the scholars of the Salaf. Abū Nu'aym collects in Al-Hilyah (8/22) the statement of Ibrāhīm Ibn Al-Ad-ham: "Looking at falsehood extensively, removes knowledge of the truth from the heart."

Ibn Wadhāh also collects in Al-Bid'ah (113) upon the authority of Hasan Al-Basrī his statement: "Do not sit with a person of innovation for it causes sickness of the heart."

Benefit of the narration: The narration (and the one that follows it) indicates that looking at and unnecessarily observing a person of innovation may cause adoration in the eyes of the beholder, particularly if the innovator is of good character and pleasant speech. This in turn lightens the affair in the heart of the beholder of the innovation he carries. As absurd as this piece of advice may seem to some in our time, it carries great wisdoms, perhaps the most prominent of them being, the preservation of one's heart. The following narration indicates that devils make the person of innovation appear fair seeming which only exacerbates the danger. See narration 181.

[١٢٢] - وَقَالَ بِشْرُ بْنُ الْحَارِثِ: إِذَا كَانَ طَرِيقُكَ عَلَى صَاحِبِ بِدْعَةٍ فَغَمِّضْ
عَيْنَيْكَ قَبْلِ أَنْ تَبْلُغَ إِلَيْهِ.

122 — Bishr Ibnil-Hārith[1] (227H) said: "If your path causes you to have to pass a person of bid'ah, then close your eyes before you reach him!"[2]

•

[١٢٣] - وَقَالَ أَبُو الْعَبَّاسِ الْخَطَّابُ: إِذَا خَرَجْتَ مِنْ بَيْتِكَ فَلَقِيَكَ صَاحِبُ
بِدْعَةٍ فَارْجِعْ فَإِنَّ الشَّيَاطِينَ مُحِيطَةٌ بِهِ.

123 — Abū 'Abbās Al-Khattāb: "If you leave from your home and you meet a person of innovation then turn back, for indeed devils are surrounding him!"[3]

•

[١٢٤] - وَقَالَ مُسْلِمُ بْنُ يَسَارٍ: إِيَّاكُمْ وَالْجِدَالَ فَإِنَّهَا سَاعَةُ جَهْلِ الْعَالِمِ وَفِيهَا
يَبْتَغِي الشَّيْطَانُ زَلَّتَهُ.

124 — Muslim Ibn Yasār (died in 100H or slightly later) said: "Be aware of argumentation, for certainly, it is a period of ignorance for the scholar, by way of it the shaytān seeks to make him slip."[4]

---

1 — He is Bishr Ibn Al-Hārith Al-Marwazī (also known as Bishr Al-Hāfī) Abū Nasr.

2 — Al-Harawī collects in *Dhammul-Kalām* (1098) the statement of 'Abdul-Wahhāb Al-Warrāq who said: "A man said to Al-Aswad Ibn Sālim: *'How is your morning?'* He replied: *'Bad! Today I laid eyes upon a person of innovation!'*"

3 — Al-Harawī collects in *Dhammul-Kalām* (833) upon the authority of Yahyā Ibn Abī Kathīr a similar statement: "If you see a person of innovation upon the path then take another one!"

4 — Collected by Ibn Battah in *Al-Ibānatul-Kubrā* (547 to 550) and Ad-Dārimī in *As-Sunan* (410).

Benefit of the narration: The narration indicates that the Salaf's warning against argumentation in the affairs of the religion was not specific to the general person but

[١٢٥] - وَقَالَ الْحَسَنُ: إِنَّ صَاحِبَ الْبِدْعَةِ لَا يُقْبَلُ لَهُ صَوْمٌ وَلَا صَلَاةٌ وَلَا حَجٌّ وَلَا عُمْرَةٌ وَلَا صَدَقَةٌ وَلَا جِهَادٌ وَلَا صَرْفٌ وَلَا عَدْلٌ.

125 — Al-Hasan said: "Indeed the person of innovation will not have his fasts, his prayer, his Hajj, his 'Umrah, his Jihād, his compulsory nor his supererogatory actions accepted."[1]

•

[١٢٦] - وَقَالَ الزُّهْرِيُّ: الِاعْتِصَامُ بِالسُّنَّةِ نَجَاةٌ وَالْعِلْمُ يُقْبَضُ قَبْضًا سَرِيعًا فَنَعْشُ الْعِلْمِ ثَبَاتُ الدِّينِ وَالدُّنْيَا وَذَهَابُ ذَلِكَ كُلِّهِ ذَهَابُ الْعُلَمَاءِ.

126 — Az-Zuhrī[2] (124H) said: "In clinging to the Sunnah is success,[3] for knowledge will be taken quickly, thus with the establishment of knowledge is the establishment of the religion and the worldly affairs, and the disappearance of all of this is in the disappearance of the 'Ulamā."[4]

---

even the scholar. When one researches the debates the scholars of the past had, they were usually out of necessity not sport.

1 — Collected by Al-Firyābī in *Al-Qadr* (376) and Al-Ājjurī in *Ash-Sharī'ah* (137). The people of knowledge hold that rejection of the righteous actions is either in regards to the actions he performs that are performed in accordance with innovation, or the actions of the innovator whose deviation is considered disbelief, in which case his actions are not accepted due to his kufr and Allāh knows best.

Benefit of the narration: The narration indicates the severe nature of the innovations that reach the level of disbelief. Narrations with wording as strong as this, are held by the people of knowledge to refer either to a severe warning (if they are used in relation to innovation that doesn't reach the level of disbelief, in order to warn individuals that they may eventually develop until they enter into what would be considered disbelief) or they apply directly to innovations of kufr.

2 — He Is Abū Bakr, Muhammad Ibn Muslim Ibn 'Abdillah Ibn 'Ubaidillah Ibn Shihāb Az-Zuhrī.

3 — i.e. Salvation in the world from being put to trial by innovated doubts, and success in the hereafter on the day of judgement.

4 — Collected by Ibn Battah in *Al-Ibānatul-Kubrā* (159 - 160) and Ad-Dārimī in *As-Sunan* (97) and Al-Lillakā'ī (136 and 137).

[١٢٧] - وَقَالَ عُمَرُ بْنُ عَبْدِ الْعَزِيزِ: مَنْ جَعَلَ دِينَهُ غَرَضًا لِلْخُصُومَاتِ - أَكْثَرَ
التَّنَقُّلَ.

127 — 'Umar Ibn 'Abdil-'Azīz said: "Whoever makes his religion
subject to argumentation, regularly changes his positions."[1]

•

[١٢٨] - وَقَالَ مُحَمَّدُ بْنُ عَلِيٍّ: لَا تُجَالِسُوا أَصْحَابَ الْخُصُومَاتِ فَإِنَّهُمْ الَّذِينَ
يَخُوضُونَ فِي آيَاتِ اللَّهِ.

128 — Muhammad Ibn 'Alī (Ibnil-Hanafīyyah) said "Do not sit
with the people who argue (and debate falsely concerning their
religion), for certainly, they are the ones who speak falsely about
the verses of Allāh."[2]

•

[١٢٩] - وَقَالَ غُضَيْفُ بْنُ الْحَارِثِ: لَا تَظْهَرُ بِدْعَةٌ إِلَّا تُرِكَ مِثْلُهَا مِنَ السُّنَّةِ.

129 — Ghudaif Ibnul-Hārith[3] (d. approx 60H) said: "No
innovation becomes apparent except that it's like from the Sunnah
is abandoned."[4]

Benefit of the narration: The narration indicates the great virtue of seeking knowledge
from its carriers before they disappear, as it also indicates the station of the people of
knowledge.

1 — Collected by Ibn Battah in *Al-Ibānatul-Kubrā'* (565, 566, 568, 569, 570).

Benefit of the narration: The narration indicates that from the evil effects of
argumentation in the affairs of religion is that the one who does so doesn't remain
firm upon the Sunnah, instead he moves from idea to idea and from denomination to
denomination.

2 — Collected by Ibn Battah in *Al-Ibānatul-Kubrā* (383, 384, 543, 553, 808) also Ad-
Dārimī (221 and 414).

3 — He is Ghudaif Ibnul-Hārith As-Sakūnī.

4 — This narration is also attributed to the Prophet (ﷺ) as his statement. It was
collected by Ahmad (4/105) and Al-Lillakā'ī (121) in its chain is Abū Bakr Ibn 'Abdullāh

[١٣٠] - وَقَالَ ابْنُ سِيرِينَ: مَا كَانَ الرَّجُلُ مَعَ الْأَثَرِ فَهُوَ عَلَى الطَّرِيقِ.

130 — Ibn Sīrīn said: "As long as a man remains upon the narrations then he remains upon the (correct) path."[1]

•

[١٣١] - وَقَالَ إِبْرَاهِيمُ: لَوْ بَلَغَنِي عَنْهُمْ - يَعْنِى الصَّحَابَةَ - أَنَّهُمْ لَمْ يُجَاوِزُوا بِالْوُضُوءِ ظُفْرًا مَا جَاوَزْتُهُ وَكَفَى عَلَى قَوْمٍ إِزْرَاءٌ أَنْ تُخَالِفَ أَعْمَالُهُمْ.

131 — Ibrāhīm (An-Nakhaʿī) said: "If it reached me that they (i.e. the companions) did not go past a fingernail when they made wudhu, I would not go past it! It is sufficient sin for a people that he opposes their actions."[2]

•

[١٣٢] - وَقَالَ شُرَيْحٌ: إِنَّمَا أَقْتَفِي الْأَثَرَ فَمَا وَجَدْتُ قَدْ سَبَقَنِي إِلَيْهِ حَدَّثْتُكُمْ بِهِ.

Ibn Abī Maryam and he is 'munkar' in hadīth (a weak narrator who opposes trustworthy narrators in that which he narrates) thus it is not established as a statement of the Prophet (صَلَّى ٱللَّٰهُ عَلَيْهِ وَسَلَّمَ). On that basis it is declared a weak hadīth by Shaikh Al-Albānī in his checking of Al-Mishkāt (1/66). It is popularly attributed to Hassān Ibn ʿAtiyyah as his statement as is collected by Ibn Wadhāh in Al-Bidʿah (90) and Ibn Battah in Al-Ibānatul-Kubrā (231).

Benefit of the narration: The narration indicates that the Sunnah is complete. Thus, anyone who carries out a bidʿah, then when he does so, he either does what the Prophet (صَلَّى ٱللَّٰهُ عَلَيْهِ وَسَلَّمَ) left in its place (which is referred to as "As-Sunnah At-Tarkiyyah" i.e. the Sunnah of the Prophet (صَلَّى ٱللَّٰهُ عَلَيْهِ وَسَلَّمَ) in leaving certain things he could have done) or he leaves what the Prophet would be doing in that place and time. So, we ultimately have replacement of the sunnah with this bidʿah. The narrations that follow fortify this affair.

1 — Collected by Ibn Battah in Al-Ibānatul-Kubrā (241 and 242) and Ad-Dārimī (142 and 143).

2 — Collected by Ad-Dārimī (218).

132 — Shuraih[1] (79H or 80H) said: "Indeed I am a follower of the narrations (of the Salaf). Whatever I have been preceded to (i.e. by someone from the pious predecessors) then I will narrate it to you."[2]

•

[١٣٣] - وَقَالَ بَعْضُ اَلْعُلَمَاءِ: وُلِدْتُ قَبْلَ الإِعْتِزَالِ.

133 — Some of the scholars said: "I was born before I'tizāl! (i.e. before the advent of the innovation of the Mu'tazilah)."

•

[١٣٤] - وَقَالَ الشَّعْبِيُّ: كُنْتُ وَلَا رَفْضَ فِي الدُّنْيَا.

134 — Ash-Sha'bi (100H) said: "I existed when there was no Rafdh[3] in the Dunyā."

•

[١٣٥] - وَذُكِرَ الْقَدَرُ عِنْدَ مُجَاهِدٍ فَقَالَ: كَفَرْتُ بِدِينٍ وُلِدْتُ قَبْلَهُ.

135 — The Innovation of Qadr was mentioned to Mujāhid (104H) and he said: "I disbelieve in a religion that I was born before!"[4]

•

---

1 — Shuraih Ibnul-Hārith Ibn Qais Al-Qādhi.

2 — Collected by Ibn Sa'd in *At-Tabaqāt* (6/136).

Benefit of the narration: The narration indicates the attitude of the Salaf was that scholarly prowess was in following the Salaf, and not in demonstrating scholarly 'creativity'. The more one knows of the knowledge of the Salaf, the greater a scholar he is. This was how they would nurture their students.

3 — Referring to the innovation of the Rāfidhah.

4 — Collected by Al-Firyābī in *Al-Qadr* (258).

Benefit of the narration: These narrations indicate that the Salaf knew that if a methodology had come about after they themselves were born, then it could not possibly be from the religion of Muhammad (صَلَّى اللهُ عَلَيْهِ وَسَلَّمَ).

[١٣٦] - وَقَالَ مَالِكُ بْنُ أَنَسٍ: قِيلَ لِرَجُلٍ عِنْدَ الْمَوْتِ عَلَى أَيِّ دَيْنٍ تَمُوتُ فَقَالَ عَلَى دِينِ أَبِي عُمَارَةَ وَكَانَ رَجُلاً يَتَوَلَّاهُ مِنْ بَعْضِ أَهْلِ الْأَهْوَاءِ، فَقَالَ مَالِكٌ رَحِمَهُ اللَّهُ: يَدَعُ دِينَ أَبِي الْقَاسِمِ وَيَمُوتُ عَلَى دِينِ أَبِي عُمَارَةَ.

136 — Imām Mālik Ibn Anas said: "It was said to a man who was at the point of death *'Which dīn will you die upon?'* So he replied: *'Upon the dīn of Abū 'Umārah!'*" (Abū 'Umārah was a man from the people of innovation.)

So Imām Mālik said concerning that: "He leaves the dīn of Abul-Qāsim (i.e. the Messenger of Allāh صَلَّى اللَّهُ عَلَيْهِ وَسَلَّمَ) and dies upon the religion of Abū 'Umārah?!"[1]

•

[١٣٧] - قَالَ: حَدَّثَنَا أَبُو الْفَضْلِ شُعَيْبُ بْنُ مُحَمَّدِ بْنِ الرَّاجِيَانِ الْكَفِيِّ قَالَ: حَدَّثَنَا عَلِيُّ بْنُ حَرْبٍ قَالَ لَنَا سُفْيَانُ بْنُ عُيَيْنَةَ عَنِ ابْنِ طَاوُوسٍ عَنْ أَبِيهِ عَنِ ابْنِ عَبَّاسٍ قَالَ: قَالَ لِي مُعَاوِيَةُ رَحْمَةُ اللَّهِ عَلَيْهِ، أَنْتَ عَلَى مِلَّةِ عَلِيٍّ رَحْمَةُ اللَّهِ عَلَيْهِ؟ قُلْتُ: لَا وَلَا عَلَى مِلَّةِ عُثْمَانَ أَنَا عَلَى مِلَّةِ رَسُولِ اللَّهِ (صَلَّى اللَّهُ عَلَيْهِ وَسَلَّمَ).

137 — It was narrated to me by Abul-Fadhl Shu'ayb Ibn Muhammad Ibnir-Rājiyān Al-Kafī, who said: it was narrated to me by 'Alī Ibn Harb: it was narrated to me by Sufyān Ibn 'Uyainah upon the authority of Tāwus upon the authority of his father upon the authority of Ibn 'Abbās (68H) — (رَضِيَ اللَّهُ عَنْهُمَا), who said: "Mu'āwiyah (may the mercy of Allāh be upon him) said to me: *'Are you upon the way of 'Alī?'* So I responded: *'No! Neither am I upon the way of 'Uthmān! I am upon the way of the Messenger of Allāh* (صَلَّى اللَّهُ عَلَيْهِ وَسَلَّمَ).'"[2]

•

---

1 — Collected by Ibn Battah in *Al-Ibānatul-Kubrā* (239).

2 — Collected by Al-Lillakā'ī (133) and Ibn Battah in *Al-Ibānatul-Kubrā* (237 and 238).

[١٣٨] - قَالَ اِبْنُ عَبَّاسٍ: مَا اِجْتَمَعَ رَجُلَانِ يَخْتَصِمَانِ فِي الدِّينِ فَافْتَرَقَا حَتَّى

يَفْتَرِيَا عَلَى اَللَّهِ عَزَّ وَجَلَّ.

138 — Ibn 'Abbās (رَضِیَاللَّهُعَنْهُمَا) said: "No two people come together and argue over the religion and then part company, without them lying upon Allāh (عَزَّوَجَلَّ)."[1]

•

[١٣٩] - وَقَالَ إِبْرَاهِيمُ النَّخَعِيُّ: مَا خَاصَمْتُ قَطُّ.

139 — Ibrāhīm An-Nakha'ī said: "I have never yet debated (i.e. about the religion)."[2]

•

[١٤٠] - وَقَالَ مُعَاذٌ: يَدُ اللَّهِ فَوْقَ الْجَمَاعَةِ وَمَنْ شَذَّ لَمْ يُبَالِ اللَّهُ بِشُذُوذِهِ.

140 — Mu'ādh said: "The Hand of Allāh is upon the Jamā'ah and whoever splits away then Allāh is not concerned with his splitting."[3]

•

---

1 — Collected by Ibn Battah in *Al-Ibānatul-Kubrā* (613).

Benefit of the narration: The narration indicates that when two people argue about the dīn then either one of them is upon truth and the other upon falsehood, in which case one of them is attributing to Allāh that which is alien to His religion, or both of them are upon falsehood in which case they both do so. If they were both upon truth they wouldn't disagree.

2 — Collected by Ibn Battah in *Al-Ibānatul-Kubrā* (631).

3 — The statement is attributed to the Prophet upon the authority of Ibn 'Umar with the wording: "The Hand of Allāh is upon the Jamā'ah and whoever splits away, then he splits away to the fire." Shaikh Al-Albānī mentions: "It is 'sahīh' up to the statement *'And whoever splits away...'*" [*Sahīh Sunan At Tirmidhi* (2167)]

Benefit of the narration: The narration indicates that the people of Sunnah are protected by Allāh and whosoever splits from the people of Sunnah then he loses Allāh's protection and harms no one but himself.

[١٤١] - وَقَالَ مُصْعَبٌ: لَا تُجَالِسْ مَفْتُونًا فَإِنَّهُ لَنْ يُخْطِئَكَ إِحْدَى اِثْنَتَيْنِ إِمَّا أَنْ يَفْتِنَكَ فَتُتَابِعَهُ أَوْ يُؤْذِيَكَ قَبْلَ أَنْ تُفَارِقَهُ.

141 — Mus'ab[1] (103H) said: "Do not sit with one who is under trial[2] in his religion since (if you do so) you will not be able to avoid one of two things: Either you will be affected by the same fitnah and thus follow him, or he will offend and harm you before you part company with him."[3]

•

[١٤٢] - وَقَالَ عَلِيٌّ كَرَّمَ اللَّهُ وَجْهَهُ: مَنْ فَارَقَ الْجَمَاعَةَ فَقَدْ خَلَعَ رِبْقَةَ الْإِسْلَامِ مِنْ عُنُقِهِ.

142 — 'Alī — May Allāh ennoble his face[4] — said: "Whoever splits from the Jamā'ah then he has removed the yoke of Islām from his neck."[5]

•

---

1 — He is Mus'ab Ibn Sa'd Ibn Abī Waqās.

2 — Meaning one who follows an innovated path

3 — Collected by Ibn Battah in Al-Ibānatul-Kubrā (385 and 433).

Benefit of the narration: The narration indicates the harm one receives from lending an ear to the people of innovation. Either your religion will be affected by his doubts or being in his presence will cause you to be harmed by what he says about what you hold dear.

4 — I have mentioned previously that it is not correct to specify 'Alī (رَضِيَ اللَّهُ عَنْهُ) with this du'ā.

5 — Collected by Ibn Battah in Al-Ibānatul-Kubrā (121). The same statement has been attributed to Ibn 'Abbās (see narration 115).

Benefit of the narration: The narration indicates that splitting from the Jamā'ah is a major sin. This strong statement refers to the grave nature of the act and that the one who falls into it is in severe danger as far as his religion is concerned since it ultimately leads to what was mentioned here.

[١٤٣] - وَقَالَ أَبُو الزُّبَيْرِ: دَخَلْتُ مَعَ طَاوُوسٍ عَلَى ابْنِ عَبَّاسٍ، فَقَالَ لَهُ طَاوُوسٌ يَا ابْنَ عَبَّاسٍ مَا تَقُولُ فِي الَّذِينَ يَرُدُّونَ الْقَدَرَ قَالَ أَرُونِي بَعْضَهُمْ قُلْنَا: صَانِعٌ مَاذَا؟ قَالَ أَنَا أَجْعَلُ يَدِي فِي رَأْسِهِ ثُمَّ أَدُقُّ عُنُقَهُ حَتَّى أَقْتُلَهُ.

143 — Abuz-Zubair (d. 126H) said: "I entered upon Ibn 'Abbās (d. 68H) – (رَضِيَاللَّهُعَنْهَا) accompanied by Tāwūs, so Tāwūs said to him: *'Oh Ibn 'Abbās what do you say about those who reject pre-decree?'* So he said: *'Show me some of them!'* So he said *'What will you do?'* He said: *'I would put my hand on his head then squeeze his neck until I kill him!'*"[1]

•

[١٤٤] - وَقَالَ ابْنُ عَبَّاسٍ: مَنْ فَارَقَ الْجَمَاعَةَ فَمَاتَ؛ مَاتَ مِيتَةً جَاهِلِيَّةً.

144 — Ibn 'Abbās said: "Whoever splits away from the Jamā'ah then dies, his death is the death of pre-Islāmic ignorance."[2]

---

1 — Collected by Ibn Battah in *Al-Ibānatul-Kubrā* (1611).

Benefit of the narration: The narration indicates how detestable this belief was to the Salaf and the harm those who propagate it cause to the ummah. Ibn Abbās was indicating by this statement how abhorrent their belief was to him and was not advocating murdering the people of innovation. Being from the greatest of the scholars among the companions of the Prophet, was well acquainted with the fact, that even if this was the legislated capital punishment for those who hold such beliefs (and it is not), it is not carried out except by the head of state, or by those whom the head of state has commissioned to carry out such affairs.

2 — Collected by Al-Khallāl in *As-Sunnah* (22). It also occurs in a hadīth attributed to the Prophet from his statement: "Whosoever sees from his leader something that displeases him then let him be patient. For indeed whoever splits from the main body (of the Muslims) a handspan and dies then his death is like the death of the pre-Islamic period." Collected by Al-Bukhārī (7054) and Muslim (1849) upon the authority of Ibn 'Abbās.

Benefit of the narration: The term Jamā'ah is a reference both to being upon the methodology of the Sunnah and being under the jurisdiction of the Muslim ruler. The one who breaks away from the jurisdiction of his ruler resembles the people of pre-Islamic times who had no ruler over them and were not united under a state. Neither were they united by one belief or opinion. Thus, this statement (which finds its origins in a hadīth of the Prophet) addresses both the issue of being in Jamā'ah referring to being united by a ruler as it refers to being united by belief, the belief of Ahlus-Sunnah.

[١٤٥] - وَقَالَ مُجَاهِدٌ فِي قَوْلِهِ - عـز وجـل - {يَخُوضُونَ فِي آيَاتِنَا} قَالَ:

«يُكَذِّبُونَ بِآيَاتِنَا.»

145 — Mujāhid said about the statement of Allāh; *"Those who engage in false conversation about our verses"*[1] — he said: "They disbelieve in the verses of Allāh."[2]

•

[١٤٦] - وَقَالَ الْحَسَنُ: وَاللَّهِ لَا يَقْبَلُ اللَّهُ مِنْ مُبْتَدِعٍ عَمَلاً يَتَقَرَّبُ بِهِ إِلَيْهِ أَبَدًا لَا صَلَاةً وَلَا صِيَامًا وَلَا زَكَاةً وَلَا حَجًّا وَلَا جِهَادًا وَلَا عُمْرَةً وَلَا صَدَقَةً حَتَّى ذَكَرَ أَنْوَاعًا مِنْ الْبِرِّ وَقَالَ إِنَّمَا مَثَلُ أَحَدِهِمْ كَمَثَلِ رَجُلٍ أَرَادَ سَفَرًا هَاهُنَا فَهَلْ يَزْدَادُ مِنْ وَجْهِهِ الَّذِي أَرَادَهُ إِلَّا بُعْدًا وَكَذَلِكَ الْمُبْتَدِعُ إِذْ لَا يَزْدَادُ بِمَا يَتَقَرَّبُ بِهِ إِلَى اللَّهِ - عـز وجـل - إِلَّا بُعْدًا.

146 — Al-Hasan: "By Allāh! Allāh will never accept from a person of innovation any action he ever does to get closer to Allāh! Not prayer nor fasting, not Zakāh nor Hajj, not Jihād nor 'Umrah or Sadaqah," — then he mentioned various forms of righteousness then said: "Indeed the example of one of you is as the example of a man who intends to embark upon a journey from here, if he travels from here (indicating a different direction) he does not increase anything but distance from his destination? Likewise, the person of innovation does not increase with the actions he does seeking nearness to Allāh in anything but being distant from Him."[3]

•

---

1 — Sūrah Al-An'ām (6):68

2 — Collected by At-Tabarī in his *Tafsīr* (7/229) and Ibn Battah in *Al-Ibānatul-Kubrā* (407, 551, 809).

3 — Collected by Al-Firyābī in *Al-Qadr* (376) and Al-Ājurrī in *Ash-Shari'ah* (64) and Al-Lillakā'ī (370).

[١٤٧] - وَقَالَ مُرَّةُ الطَّيِّبُ فِي قَوْلِهِ (تَعَالَى) {وَأَفْئِدَتُهُمْ هَوَاءٌ} قَالَ: «مُنْحَرِفَةٌ
عَنِ الْحَقِّ لَا تَعِي شَيْئًا.»

147 — Murratut-Tayyib[1] (90H) said concerning the statement of
Allāh; "...and their hearts (are) a gaping void"[2] — he said: "(Their hearts)
have deviated from the truth thus they understand nothing."[3]

•

[١٤٨] - وَقَالَ أَبُو حَمْزَةَ سَأَلْتُ إِبْرَاهِيمَ عَنْ هَذِهِ الْأَهْوَاءِ أَيُّهَا أَعْجَبُ إِلَيْكَ
فَإِنِّي أُحِبُّ أَنْ آخُذَ بِرَأْيِكَ فَقَالَ مَا جَعَلَ اللَّهُ فِي شَيْءٍ مِنْهَا مِثْقَالَ ذَرَّةٍ مِنْ
خَيْرٍ وَمَا هِيَ إِلَّا زِينَةٌ مِنَ الشَّيْطَانِ وَمَا الْأَمْرُ إِلَّا الْأَمْرُ الْأَوَّلُ.

148 — Abū Hamzah[4] said: "I asked Ibrāhīm[5] concerning which
type of desires he inclines towards, as I wished to take his opinion,
so he said: 'Indeed Allāh has not put an atoms weight of good in
it (i.e. desires). Indeed, it is nothing but the beautifications of the
Shaytān, the (upright) affair is the first affair (i.e. that which the first
generations were upon).'"[6]

•

---

1 — He is Murrah Ibn Sharāhīl Al-Hamdānī.

2 — Sūrah Ibrāhīm (33):43

The āyah refers to their hearts being void of understanding, thus resembling a literal
empty void.

3 — Collected By Ibn Abī Shaibah in *Al-Musannaf* (34884) and At-Tabarī in *At-Tafsīr*
(13/240) with the wording " متخرفة (their hearts are deluded...)".

4 — He is Abū Hamzah Al-Qassāb, Maimūn Al-Aʿwar Al-Kūfī and he is weak in
hadīth.

5 — i.e. Ibrāhīm An-Nakhaʿī

6 — Collected by Abū Nuʿaym in *Al-Hilyah* (4/222) and Ibn Abī Zamanīn in *Riyādhul-
Jannah* (230: Maktabatul Ghurabā Print).

Benefit of the narration: The narration indicates the great station of these two affairs. [1]
Guidance to the truth. [2] Guidance upon the truth.

[١٤٩] - وَقَالَ أَبُو اَلْعَالِيَةِ: نِعْمَتَانِ لِلَّهِ عَلَيَّ لَا أَدْرِي أَيُّهُمَا أَفْضَلُ أَوْ قَالَ

أَعْظَمُ: أَنْ هَدَانِي لِلْإِسْلَامِ وَالْأُخْرَى أَنْ عَصَمَنِي مِنْ اَلرَّافِضَةِ.

149 — Abul-'Āliyah said: "There are two blessings upon me from
Allāh, I do not know which of the two is better (or he said greater).
(The first being) that Allāh has guided me to Islām and the other
that Allāh has saved me from the Rāfidhah."[1]

•

[١٥٠] - وَقَالَ اَلْحَسَنُ بْنُ شَقِيقٍ كُنَّا عِنْدَ اِبْنِ الْمُبَارَكِ إِذْ جَاءَهُ رَجُلٌ فَقَالَ لَهُ

أَنْتَ ذَاكَ الْجَهْمِيُّ قَالَ نَعَمْ. قَالَ إِذَا خَرَجْتَ مِنْ عِنْدِي فَلَا تَعُدْ إِلَيَّ. قَالَ

اَلرَّجُلُ فَأَنَا تَائِبٌ. قَالَ لَا حَتَّى يَظْهَرَ مِنْ تَوْبَتِكَ مِثْلُ اَلَّذِي ظَهَرَ مِنْ بِدْعَتِكَ.

150 — Al-Hasan Ibn Shaqīq said: "We were in the presence of
Ibnil-Mubārak when a man came to him, so he said: *'Aren't you that
Jahmi?'* He said: *'Yes,'* so he said: *'When you leave from here then do not
return to me!'* He replied: *'I repent!'*

So he said: 'Not until there manifests of your taubah the like of that
which was manifest of your innovation!'"[2]

---

1 — Collected by Ibn Sa'd in *At-Tabaqāt* (7/114) and Al-Harawī in *Dhammul-Kalām*
(793) with the wording: "I do not know which of the (following) two blessings upon me
are greatest. That Allāh took me from Shirk to Islām, or that Allāh protected me in
Islām from having desires" — and Abū Nu'aym in *Al-Hilyah* (2/218) and Al-Baihaqī in
Shu'abul-Īmān (3508).

2 — Benefit of the narration: The narration indicates the position of the Salaf in regards
to boycotting the people of innovation. It also points towards the fact repentance from
innovations has conditions that are made clear in the statement of Allāh: *"Indeed, those
who conceal what We sent down of clear proofs and guidance after We made it clear for the people
in the Scripture — those are cursed by Allāh and cursed by those who curse. Except for those who
repent and correct themselves and make evident [what they concealed]. Those: I will accept their
repentance, and I am the Accepting of repentance, the Merciful."* [2: 159-160]

The people of knowledge apply the verse to the one who repents from innovation. In it
are conditions for his repentance being accepted. [1] Taubah, that is he repents to Allāh.
[2] That he corrects himself and whatever he may have carried out from propagating

[١٥١] - وَقَالَ بَقِيَّةُ بْنُ الْوَلِيدِ: قَالَ لِي ثَابِتُ بْنُ عَجْلَانَ أَدْرَكْتُ أَنَسٍ بْنَ

مَالِكٍ وَسَعِيدَ بْنَ اَلْمُسَيِّبِ وَعَامِرًا الشَّعْبِيَّ وَسَعِيدَ بْنَ جُبَيْرٍ وَالْحَكَمَ بْنَ عُتَيْبَةَ

وَحَمَّادَ بْنَ أَبِي سُلَيْمَانَ وَعَطَاءً وَطَاوُوسًا وَمُجَاهِدًا وَابْنَ أَبِي مُلَيْكَةَ وَمَكْحُولاً

وَسُلَيْمَانَ بْنَ مُوسَى وَالْحَسَنَ وَابْنَ سِيرِينَ وَأَبَا عَامِرٍ مَعَ غَيْرِهِمْ قَدْ سَمَّاهُمْ.

فَكُلُّهُمْ يَأْمُرُنِي بِالصَّلَاةِ فِي جَمَاعَةٍ وَيَنْهَانِي عَنِ الْأَهْوَاءِ وَالْبِدَعِ حَتَّى

قَالَ: وَقَالَ لِي: «يَا أَبَا مُحَمَّدٍ وَاللَّهِ مَا مِنْ عَمَلِي شَيْءٌ أُوْثَقُ فِي نَفْسِي مِنْ

مِشْيَتِي إِلَى هَذَا اَلْمَسْجِدِ وَلَرُبَّمَا كَانَ عَلَيْهِ الْوَالِي كَمَا شَاءَ اللَّهُ أَنْ يَكُونَ قَدْ

عَرَفْنَا ذَلِكَ مِنْهُ وَرَأَيْنَاهُ فَلَا نَدَعُ اَلصَّلَاةَ خَلْفَهُ.»

151 — Baqiyyah Ibnil-Walīd[1] (197H) said: "Thābit Ibn ʿAjlān[2] (d. between 131H and 140H) said to me: 'I met Anas Ibn Mālik, Saʿīd Ibn Musayyib[3] (d. after 90H), ʿĀmir (d. 121H), Ash-Shaʿbi (d. 100H), Saʿīd Ibn Jubair (d. 95H), Al-Hakam Ibn ʿUtaibah[4] (d. 113H), Hamād Ibn Abī Sulaimān, ʿAtāʾ (d. 114H), Tāwūs (d. 106H), Mujāhid, Ibn Abī Mulaikah[5] (d. 117H), Makhūl[6] (d. after 110H), Sulaimān Ibn Mūsā,[7] Al-Hasan (d. 110H), Ibn Sīrīn (d. 110H), Abā ʿĀmir (who met Abū Bakr As-Siddīq رضي الله عنه as well as other individuals)' — he mentioned: 'All of them commanded me with Salāh in congregation and prohibited me from desires and innovation.'

---

falsehood, he rectifies what he had previously done. [3] He clarifies, declares and makes apparent his rectification publicly, this is the one whose repentance will be accepted. Thus we see in this narration the implementation of the Salaf of these verses of the Qurʾān.

1 — He is Baqiyyah Ibn Walīd Ibn Sāʿid Al-Kalāʿī.

2 — He is Thābit Ibn ʿAjlān Al-Ansārī.

3 — He is Saʿīd Ibn Masayyib Al-Makhzūmī.

4 — He is Al-Hakam Ibn ʿUtaibah Al-Kindi Al-Kūfī.

5 — He is Abū Bakr ʿAbdullāh Ibn ʿUbaidillāh Ibn Abī Mulaikah Al-Qurashī At-Taimī.

6 — He is Makhūl Ash-Shāmī, Abū ʿAbdillāh.

7 — He is Sulaimān Ibn Mūsā Al-Amawi Ad-Dimishqī.

Then he said to me: 'Oh Abū Muḥammad! By Allāh! None of my righteous actions is more significant to me, than my walking to the masjid. And perhaps a governor would be upon that which Allāh willed him to be upon (i.e. from sin), and we would know this from him and observe it, yet that would not prevent us from praying behind him.'"[1]

•

[١٥٢] - وَقَالَ ابْنُ وَهْبٍ: سُئِلَ مَالِكٌ عَنْ أَهْلِ الْقَدَرِ أَيُكَفُّ عَنْ كَلَامِهِمْ أَوْ

خُصُومَتِهِمْ أَفْضَلُ قَالَ نَعَمْ إِذَا كَانَ عَارِفًا بِمَا هُوَ عَلَيْهِ قَالَ وَتَأْمُرُهُ بِالْمَعْرُوفِ

وَتَنْهَاهُ عَنِ الْمُنْكَرِ وَتُخْبِرُهُمْ بِخِلَافِهِمْ. وَلَا يُرَاضَعُوا وَلَا تُصَلِّي خَلْفَهُمْ قَالَ

مَالِكٌ وَلَا أَرَى أَنْ يُنَاكَحُوا

152 — Ibn Wahb said: Imām Mālik was asked concerning the people of Qadr (i.e. the people who had fallen into innovation concerning belief in pre-decree); does one refrain from speaking to them or is it better to debate with them? He said: "Yes — if he is acquainted with that which he is upon!"

He said (continuing): "And he commands him with good and forbids him from evil and informs them of their opposition (i.e. to the Sunnah). Though they are not to be debated with, neither does one pray behind."

Mālik then said: "And I do not see that they may be married."[2]

•

---

1 — Collected by Al-Lillakā'ī (239) and At-Tabarānī in *Musnad Ash-Shāmiyīn* (2257) and Al-Fasawī in *Al-Ma'rifah* (3/375).

Benefit of the narration: The narration indicates the great station clinging to the main body of Ahlus-Sunnah, and not splitting from them in belief and action. And from the greatest of their actions, them coming together for congregational prayer.

2 — Collected by Ibn Battah in *Al-Ibānatul-Kubrā* (1861) and mentioned by Qādhi 'Iyādh in *Tartībul-Madārik* (1/91).

[١٥٣] - قَالَ: وَسُئِلَ مَالِكٌ عن تَزْوِيجِ القَدَرِيِّ فَقَالَ: {وَلَعَبْدٌ مُّؤْمِنٌ خَيْرٌ مِّن مُّشْرِكٍ.} البقرة: ٢٢١

153 — Imām Mālik was asked about marrying a Qadarī? He responded [quoting the verse in the Qur'an; 2:221]: "A believing slave is better (to marry) than a Mushrik."[1]

[١٥٤] - قَالَ وَسَمِعْتُ مَالِكًا يَقُولُ كَانَ ذَلِكَ الرَّجُلُ إِذَا جَاءَهُ بَعْضُ هَؤُلَاءِ أَصْحَابِ الْأَهْوَاءِ قَالَ: «أَمَّا أَنَا فَعَلَى بَيِّنَةٍ مِنْ رَبِّي وَأَمَّا أَنْتَ فَشَاكٌّ فَاذْهَبْ إِلَى شَاكٍّ مِثْلِكَ فَخَاصِمْهُ»

154 — He (Ibn Wahb) said: "I heard Mālik say: 'That individual[2] would say to the people of desires when they would come to debate with him *As for me then I am upon clear-sightedness with my religion as for you then you have doubt so go and debate with a doubtful person like yourself!*'"[3]

[١٥٥] - قَالَ وَقَالَ مَالِكٌ: يَلْبِسُونَ عَلَى أَنْفُسِهِمْ وَيَطْلُبُونَ مَنْ يَعِرِّفُهُمْ.

---

1 — Collected by Ibn Abī 'Āsim in *As-Sunnah* (198) and Ibn Battah in *Al-Ibānatul-Kubrā* (1859) and Al-Lillakā'ī (1352).

Benefit of the narration: The narration indicates that the Salaf held the Qadariyah to be Kuffār. This was majorly due to their denial of the knowledge of Allāh. The Qadariyah claim that Allāh does not know of the actions of the servant until they perform them and in believing this they deny one of the most commonly established attributes of Allāh that of His knowledge. Thus we see these statements of Imām Mālik revolve around him holding them to be Kuffār.

2 — Translator's Note: And perhaps he intended Al-Hasan Al-Basrī when he said *"that individual."*

3 — Collected by Abū Nu'aym in *Al-Hilyah* (6/324) and Ibn Battah in *Al-Ibānatul-Kubrā* (307).

155 — He (Ibn Wahb) said: "Mālik said: 'They confuse themselves, and then they seek out those who will acquaint them (with their dīn).'"[1]

•

[١٠٦] - وَقَالَ مَالِكٌ: قَالَ لِي رَجُلٌ «لَقَدْ دَخَلْتُ فِي هَذِهِ الْأَدْيَانَ كُلَّهَا فَلَمْ أَرَ شَيْئًا مُسْتَقِيمًا فَقَالَ لَهُ رَجُلٌ مِنْ أَهْلِ اَلْمَدِينَةِ مِن الْمُتَكَلِّمِينَ فَأَنَا أُخْبِرُكَ لِمَ ذَلِكَ» قَالَ قُلْتُ «لِأَنَّكَ لَا تَتَّقِي اللَّهَ وَلَوْ كُنْتَ تَتَّقِي اللَّهَ لَجَعَلَ لَكَ مِنْ أَمْرِكَ مَخْرَجًا»

156 — Mālik said: "A man said to me: 'I have looked into the affair of all of these religions, and I do not see anything upright from them!'

So a man of theological rhetoric from the people of Madīnah said (to him) 'I shall inform you of why that is?'"

So he (Mālik) said: "I said (interjecting): 'Because you don't fear Allāh, If you had feared Allāh, He would have made a way out of your affair for you (i.e. guided you).'"[2]

•

[١٠٧] - وَقَالَ أَبُو سُهَيْلٍ «عَمُّ مَالِكٍ بْنِ أَنَسٍ» شَاوَرَنِي عُمَرُ بْنُ عَبْدِ الْعَزِيزِ فِي الْقَدَرِيَّةِ فَقُلْتُ: «أَرَى أَنْ تَسْتَتِيبَهُمْ فَإِنْ تَابُوا وَإِلَّا ضَرَبْتَهُمْ بِالسَّيْفِ» فَقَالَ عُمَرُ «ذَاكَ رَأْيِي وَكَذَلِكَ» كَانَ يَرَى مَالِكُ بْنُ أَنَسٍ وَالْحَسَنُ فِيهِمْ.»

---

1 — Collected by Ibn 'Abdil-Hakam in *Al-Jāmi'* (166) and Ibn Battah in *Al-Ibānatul-Kubrā* (307).

2 — Collected by Ibn Battah in *Al-Ibānatul-Kubrā* (313).

157 — Abū Suhail the uncle of Mālik Ibn Anas[1] (died after 140H) said: "'Umar Ibn Abdil-'Azīz consulted with me regarding the Qadariyyah he said: *'I see that repentance should be sought from them, then either they repent or they should be struck with the sword.'* 'Umar said: *'And that is my opinion,'* and that was likewise the view of Mālik Ibn Anas and Al-Hasan."[2]

•

[١٥٨] - وَكَانَ الْحَسَنُ بْنُ مُحَمَّدِ بْنِ عَلِيٍّ لَا يَرَاهُمْ مُسْلِمِينَ وَكَذَلِكَ الْخَوَارِجُ.

158 — Al-Hasan Ibn Muhammad Ibn 'Alī did not consider them (i.e. the Qadariyah) as Muslims, and similarly the Khawārij.[3]

•

[١٥٩] - وَقَالَ ابْنُ الْمُبَارَكِ: مَنْ تَعَاطَى الْكَلَامَ تَزَنْدَقَ.

---

1 — Some prints mention Anas Ibn Mālik, this is an error, as is established in the sources of the narration and in the sources that mention the biography of Abū Suhail, whose name was Nāfi' Ibn Mālik Ibn Abī 'Āmir Al-Asbahī, thus I have amended the text accordingly. See: *Tārīkhul-Kabīr* of Imāmul-Bukhārī (8/86) and *At-Tārīkh* of Muhammad Ibn Ahmad Al-Muqadamī (114) and *Al-Istighnā* of Ibn 'Abdil-Barr (2/935). From the clearest evidence of that is the statement of Ibn Battah himself when he collects the narration in *Al-Ibānatul-Kubrā* (1834) mentioning the statement of one of the narrators within the chain of transmission, Qutaibah Ibn Sa'īd who said: "Mālik Ibn Anas narrated to us from his uncle; Abū Suhail Ibn Mālik…"

2 — Collected by Ibn Abī 'Āsim in *As-Sunnah* (197-199) and Al-Khallāl in *As-Sunnah* (876) and Al-Firyābī in *Al-Qadr* (243) and Al-Ājjurī in *Ash-Shari'ah* (216).

Benefit of the narration: The narration indicates that the Salaf saw that capital punishment should be established upon the Qadariyah due to their disbelief. 'Umar Ibn 'Abdil-'Azīz was the Khalīfah at the time and he sought the counsel of the major scholars concerning how they should be dealt with. They all agreed upon the establishment of capital punishment upon those who are persistent from them.

3 — Benefit of the narration: The narration indicates that the scholars of the Salaf held the Qadariyah to be kuffār. From them was a group who held the same view, though there is some difference concerning whether or not the khawārij are considered kuffār.

159 — Ibn Mubārak said: "Whoever resorts to rhetoric becomes a heretic."[1]

•

[١٦٠] - وَقَالَ ابْنُ الْمُبَارَكِ: إِنَّ لِلَّهِ مَلَائِكَةً يَطْلُبُونَ حِلَقَ الذِّكْرِ فَانْظُرْ مَعَ مَنْ يَكُونُ مَجْلِسُكَ، لَا يَكُونُ مَعَ صَاحِبِ بِدْعَةٍ، فَإِنَّ اللَّهَ لَا يَنْظُرُ إِلَيْهِمْ وَعَلَامَةُ النِّفَاقِ أَنْ يَقُومَ الرَّجُلُ وَيَقْعُدَ مَعَ صَاحِبِ بِدْعَةٍ.

160 — Ibn Al-Mubārak said: "Indeed Allāh has angels who seek out circles of remembrance, so look to who you sit with, do not accompany people of innovation for indeed Allāh does not look at them. A sign of hypocrisy is that one sits and stands with the people of innovation."[2]

•

[١٦١] - وَقَالَ مُحَمَّدُ بْنُ النَّضْرِ الْحَارِثِيُّ: مَنْ أَصْغَى بِسَمْعِهِ إِلَى صَاحِبِ بِدْعَةٍ نُزِعَتْ مِنْهُ الْعِصْمَةُ وَوُكِلَ إِلَى نَفْسِهِ.

161 — Muhammad Ibn Nadhr Al-Hārithī[3] said: "Whoever pays attention to a person of innovation, will have the protection of Allāh removed from him, and will be left to his own devices."[4]

---

1 — Al-Harawī collects upon the authority of Imām Malik (873) his statement: "Whosoever seeks (knowledge of) the religion through theoretical rhetoric becomes a heretic."

Benefit of the narration: The narration indicates the position of the Salaf in relation to the usage of philosophical theological rhetoric. They held that it leads to heresy in the religion.

2 — The author collects this statement upon the authority of Fudhail Ibn 'Iyādh (438) also Al-Lillakā'ī (265) it would appear this is what is correct — and Allāh knows best.

3 — He is Muhammad Ibn Nadhr Al-Hārithī Al-Kūfī.

4 — Collected by Al-Lillakā'ī (252) and Al-Harawī in Dhammul-Kalām (934) with the wording: "Whoever pays attention to a person of innovation leaves the protection of Allāh." Al-Harawī attributes the version mention above Yūsuf Ibn Asbāt (934).

[١٦٢] - وَقَالَ الْفُضَيْلُ بْنُ عِيَاضٍ: أَدْرَكْتُ خِيَارَ النَّاسِ كُلُّهُمْ أَصْحَابُ

سُنَّةٍ يَنْهَوْنَ عَنْ أَصْحَابِ الْبِدَعِ، وَصَاحِبُ سُنَّةٍ وَإِنْ قَلَّ عَمَلُهُ فَإِنِّي أَرْجُو لَهُ

وَصَاحِبُ بِدْعَةٍ لَا يَرْفَعُ اللَّهُ لَهُ عَمَلاً وَإِنْ كَثُرَ.

162 — Fudhail Ibn 'Iyādh said: "I met the best of people all of them
companions of Sunnah, they would warn against the people of
innovation. The companion of Sunnah, even if his actions are few,
I have good hopes for him. As for the companion of bid'ah, then
Allāh does not raise any of his actions even if they are abundant."[1]

•

[١٦٣] - وَقَالَ عَبْدُ اللَّهِ بْنُ عُمَرَ السَّرْخَسِيُّ عَالِمُ الْحَرَنِ صَاحِبُ ابْنِ المُبَارَكِ

أَكَلْتُ عِنْدَ صَاحِبِ بِدْعَةٍ أَكْلَةً فَبَلَغَ ابْنَ المُبَارَكِ فَقَالَ: «لَا أُكَلِّمُكَ ثَلَاثِينَ

يَوْمًا».

163 — 'Abdullāh Ibn 'Umar As-Sarkhasī the scholar of Haran[2] and
companion of Ibnil-Mubārak[3] (181H) said: "I ate some food with a
person of innovation on an occasion and it reached Ibnil-Mubārak
so he said: *I will not speak to you for thirty days!*"[4]

•

1 — Collected by Al-Lillakā'ī (267).

2 — This is other than Harān, it refers to a region also known as Darān or Kirmān in
present day Iran.

3 — He is 'Abdullāh Ibn Al-Mubārak Al-Marwazī, it was said about him: "He gathered
all the characteristics of khair (goodness)."

4 — Collected by Al-Lillakā'ī (274) and Ibn Hibbān In *Ath-Thiqāt* (8/350).

Benefit of the narration: The narration indicates that the Salaf would even boycott the
person of Sunnah who spent time with the people of innovation in order to discipline
them.

[١٦٤] - وَقَالَ إِسْمَاعِيلُ الطُّوسِيُّ: قَالَ لِي اِبْنُ اَلْمُبَارَكِ «يَكُونُ مَجْلِسُكَ مَعَ المَسَاكِينِ وَإِيَّاكَ أَنْ يَكُونَ مَجْلِسُكَ مَعَ صَاحِبٍ بِدْعَةٍ فَإِنِّي أَخْشَى عَلَيْكَ مَقْتَ اللَّهِ عَزَّ وَجَلَّ.»

164 — Ismāʿīl At-Tūsī said: "Ibnil-Mubārak said to me 'Let your sittings be with the poor and beware of sitting with the companion of innovation, for indeed I fear for you the anger of Allāh (عَزَّوَجَلَّ).'"[1]

•

[١٦٥] - وَقَالَ الْفُضَيْلُ: إِيَّاكَ أَنْ تَجْلِسَ مَعَ صَاحِبٍ بِدْعَةٍ فَإِنِّي أَخْشَى عَلَيْكَ مَقْتَ اللَّهِ - عَزَّ وَجَلَّ.

165 — Fudhail (Ibn ʿIyādh) said: "Beware of sitting with a person of innovation, for indeed I fear for you the anger of Allāh (عَزَّوَجَلَّ)."

•

[١٦٦] - وَقَالَ مَنْصُورُ بْنُ اَلْمُعْتَمِرِ: بَعَثَ اللَّهُ آدَمَ عَلَيْهِ اَلسَّلَامُ بِالشَّرِيعَةِ فَكَانَ اَلنَّاسُ عَلَى شَرِيعَةِ آدَمَ حَتَّى ظَهَرَتْ الزَّنْدَقَةُ فَذَهَبَتْ شَرِيعَةُ آدَمَ ثُمَّ بَعَثَ اللَّهُ نُوحًا عَلَيْهِ اَلسَّلَامُ بِالشَّرِيعَةِ فَكَانَ اَلنَّاسُ عَلَى شَرِيعَةِ نُوحٍ فَمَا أَذْهَبَهَا إِلَّا الزَّنْدَقَةُ ثُمَّ بَعَثَ اللَّهُ إِبْرَاهِيمَ عَلَيْهِ اَلسَّلَامُ فَكَانَ النَّاسُ عَلَى شَرِيعَةِ إِبْرَاهِيمَ عَلَيْهِ السَّلَامُ حَتَّى ظَهَرَتْ الزَّنْدَقَةُ فَذَهَبَتْ شَرِيعَةُ إِبْرَاهِيمَ عَلَيْهِ السَّلَامُ ثُمَّ بَعَثَ اللَّهُ - عَزَّ وَجَلَّ - مُوسَى عَلَيْهِ السَّلَامُ فَكَانَ النَّاسُ عَلَى شَرِيعَةِ مُوسَى حَتَّى ظَهَرَتْ الزَّنْدَقَةُ فَذَهَبَتْ شَرِيعَةُ مُوسَى ثُمَّ بَعَثَ اللَّهُ عَلَيْهِ اَلسَّلَامُ عِيسَى فَكَانَ النَّاسُ عَلَى شَرِيعَةِ

---

1 — Collected by Al-Lillakāʾī (260) and Ibn Battah in *Al-Ibānatul-Kubrā* (452) and Abū Nuʿaym in *Al-Hilyah* (8/168).

عِيسَى حَتَّى ظَهَرَتِ الزَّندقةُ، فَذَهَبَتْ شَرِيعَةُ عِيسَى، ثُمَّ بَعَثَ اللَّهُ محمـدًا بِالشَّرِيعَةِ فَلَا يُخَافُ عَلَى ذَهَابِ هَذَا الدِّينِ إِلَّا بِالزَّنْدَقَةِ.

166 — Mansūr Ibnil Mu'tamir[1] (132H) said: "Allāh sent Ādam with a Shari'ah, thus the people were upon the Shari'ah of Ādam until heresy appeared, and the Shari'ah of Ādam disappeared.

Then Allāh sent Nūh (Noah) with the Shari'ah, and thus the people were upon the Shari'ah of Nūh, and nothing caused it to disappear other than heresy.

Then Allāh sent Ibrāhīm (عَلَيْهِالسَّلَامُ) with the Shari'ah, so the people were upon the Shari'ah of Ibrāhīm until heresy appeared, thus the Shari'ah of Ibrāhīm disappeared.

Then Allāh sent Mūsā (عَلَيْهِالسَّلَامُ), and the people remained upon the Shari'ah of Mūsā until heresy appeared, and so the Shari'ah of Mūsā disappeared. Then Allāh sent 'Īsā (عَلَيْهِالسَّلَامُ), and the people were upon the Shari'ah of 'Īsā until heresy appeared and the Shari'ah of 'Īsā disappeared.

Then Allāh sent Muhammad (صَلَّىاللَّهُعَلَيْهِوَسَلَّمَ) with the Shari'ah and there is nothing that is feared that will cause this religion to disappear other than heresy."[2]

•

[١٦٧] - وَقَالَ مُحَمَّدُ بْنُ عَلِيٍّ: لَا تُطِيعُوا رُؤَسَاءَ الدُّنْيَا فَيُنْسَخَ الدِّينَ مِنْ قُلُوبِكُمْ.

---

1 — He is Mansūr Ibn Mu'tamir Ibn 'Abdillāh As-Sumalī, Abū 'Itāb Al-Kūfī.

2 — Collected by At-Tabarānī in *Al-Awsat* (8/204) and Al-Harawī in *Dhammul-Kalām* (57) from the statement of Zaid Ibn Rufai' slightly abbreviated.

Benefit of the narration: The narration indicates that it was innovation in the religion that caused the previous religions to become corrupt. Successful indeed is the one that takes lessons from the past.

167 — Muhammad Ibn 'Alī said: "Do not obey the leaders of the Dunyā (i.e those at the forefront of striving for it) and thus the religion will be removed from your hearts."

•

[١٦٨] - وَقَالَ الشَّعْبِيُّ: إِذَا أَطَاعَ النَّاسُ سُلْطَانَهُمْ فِيمَا يَبْتَدِعُ لَهُمْ أَخْرَجَ اللَّهُ مِنْ قُلُوبِهِمْ الإِيمَانَ وَأَسْكَنَهَا الرُّعْبَ.

168 — Ash-Sha'bī[1] (100H) said: "If the people obey their leaders in that which they innovate for them, Allāh will remove Īmān from their hearts and cause fear to dwell within them."[2]

•

[١٦٩] - وَقَالَ الحَسَنُ: سَيَأْتِي أُمَرَاءُ يَدْعُونَ النَّاسَ إِلَى مُخَالَفَةِ السُّنَّةِ فَتُطِيعُهُمْ الرَّعِيَّةُ خَوْفًا عَلَى ذَهَابِ دُنْيَاهُمْ فَعِنْدَهَا سَلَبَهُمْ اللَّهُ الإِيمَانَ وَأَوْرَثَهُمْ اَلْفَقْرَ وَنَزَعَ مِنْهُمْ الصَّبْرَ وَلَمْ يَأْجُرْهُمْ عَلَيْهِ.

169 — Al-Hasan said: "There will come leaders who will call the people to oppose the Sunnah, and so their subjects will obey them, fearing the disappearance of their Dunya, and it is then that Allāh will strip their hearts of Īmān and replace it with poverty. Patience will be lifted from them, and thus they will not be rewarded for it."

•

---

1 — He is 'Āmir Ibn Sharāhīl, Abū 'Amr Al-Kūfī.

2 — Benefit of the narration: The narration (and the one that follows) indicate that the Salaf understood that obedience to the ruler is in that which is considered good, he is not to be obeyed upon sin and transgression. In fact, obeying him in innovation in the religion, is a cause for doubts to fester in the hearts and the religion to become corrupt particularly for the future generations (see narration 174 as a clear example), ultimately the subjects will become despondent in regards to their ruler, leading to the descension of the state itself. (Also see 175 and 177)

[١٧٠] - وَقَالَ يُونُسُ بْنُ عُبَيْدٍ: إِذَا خَالَفَ السُّلْطَانُ السُّنَّةَ وَقَالَتِ الرَّعِيَّةُ قَدْ أُمِرْنَا بِطَاعَتِهِ أَسْكَنَ اللَّهُ قُلُوبَهُمُ الشَّكَّ وَأَوْرَثَهُمُ التَّطَاعُنَ.

170 — Yūnus Ibn 'Ubaid[1] (139H) said: "If the ruler opposes the Sunnah, and his subjects say: 'We have been commanded to obey', Allāh will cause doubt to dwell in their hearts, and He will make defamation (of the ruler) be their lot."

•

[١٧١] - وَقَالَ النَّبِيُّ (صَلَّى اللَّهُ عَلَيْهِ وَسَلَّمَ): «دِينُ الْمَرْءِ عَلَى دِينِ خَلِيلِهِ فَلْيَنْظُرْ أَحَدُكُمْ مَنْ يُخَالِلِ.» وَقَالَ سُلَيْمَانُ بْنُ دَاوُدَ «لَا تَحْكُمُوا عَلَى أَحَدٍ بِشَيْءٍ حَتَّى تَنْظُرُوا مَنْ يُخَادِنُ.»

171 — The Prophet (صَلَّى اللَّهُ عَلَيْهِ وَسَلَّمَ) said: "A man is upon the religion of his friend so let one of you look to who he befriends." Sulaimān Ibn Dāwūd said: "Do not pass judgement upon anyone with anything until you look to his associates."[2]

•

[١٧٢] - وَأَوْحَى اللَّهُ - عَزَّ وَجَلَّ - إِلَى مُوسَى: «يَا مُوسَى كُنْ يَقْظَانًا وَارْتَدْ لِنَفْسِكَ إِخْوَانًا وَكُلُّ خِدْنٍ لَا يُوَاتِيكَ عَلَى مَسَرَّتِي فَاحْذَرْهُ فَإِنَّهُ لَكَ عَدُوٌّ وَأَنَا مِنْهُ بَرِيءٌ.»

172 — Allāh revealed to Mūsā saying: "Oh Mūsā! Be alert! And choose for yourself (good) brothers (associates). Any companion

---

1 — He is Yūnus Ibn 'Ubaid Ibn Dinār Al-'Abdi, Abū 'Abdillāh.

2 — Collected by the author in Al-Ibānatul-Kubrā (359 and 362).

Benefit of the narration: The narration and the one that follows, indicate that the Salaf understood that a person is judged by his companions, since people ordinarily accompany individuals similar to themselves in nature and belief.

that doesn't favourably aid you in pleasing me, then beware of him, for certainly, he is your enemy and I am free of him."[1]

•

[١٧٣] - وَقَالَ ابْنُ الْمُبَارَكِ: مَنْ خَفِيَتْ عَلَيْنَا بِدْعَتُهُ لَمْ تَخْفَ عَلَيْنَا أَسَالِفَته.

173 — Ibnul-Mubārak said: "He whose innovation may be hidden from us then his companionship will not be hidden from us."[2]

•

[١٧٤] - وَقِيلَ إِنَّهُ كَانَ لِلْمَجُوسِ دِينٌ وَكِتَابٌ فَوَقَعَ مَلِكٌ مِنْهُمْ عَلَى أُخْتِهِ وَقَدْ كَانَ هَوِيَهَا فَخَافَ رَعِيَّتَهُ فَقَالَ «إِنَّ الَّذِي صَنَعْتُ حَلَالٌ ثُمَّ قَتَلَهُمْ عَلَى ذَلِكَ فَظَهَرَ عَلَيْهِمْ حَتَّى بَقِيَ فِي الْمَجُوسِ نِكَاحُ الْأَخَوَاتِ وَالْأُمَّهَاتِ وَبَطَلَتْ شَرِيعَتُهُمُ الْأُولَى.»

174 — It was said that the Magians had a religion and a book until a king (from among them) had relations with a sister of his that he used to desire. (After that occurred) he feared what his subjects would say, so he declared: "That which I have done is halāl (permissible) then he fought against them due to this and was victorious. Thus, due to this, marrying sisters or mothers remained among them and the Sharī'ah they were given was nullified."[3]

•

[١٧٥] - وَقَالَ الْحَسَنُ: لَا يَزَالُ هَذَا الدِّينُ مَتِينًا مَا لَمْ تَقَعِ الْأَهْوَاءُ فِي السُّلْطَانِ هُمُ الَّذِينَ يَدِينُونَ النَّاسَ فَإِذَا وَقَعَ فِيهِمْ فَمَنْ يَدِينُهُمْ.

1 — Collected by Ahmad in Az-Zuhd (p.85) and Ibn Abī Dunyā in Ash-Shukr (164) and Ibn 'Asākir in At-Tārīkh (61/153) and the author in Al-Ibānatul-Kubrā (366).

2 — Collected by Ibn Abī Dunyā in Al-Ikhwān (40) and Al-Lillakā'ī (257).

3 — Collected by 'Abdur-Razzāq in Al-Mussanaf (19262) and Ash-Shāfi'ī in Al-Musnad (p.170) and Al-Baihaqī in Al-Ibānatul-Kubrā (9/188).

175 — Al-Ḥasan said: "This religion will not cease being strong, as long as the people do not start following their desire in relation to the ruler. For they (the rulers) are those who govern and protect the religion of the people, thus if they stand against them (i.e. if the common folk stand against the ruler) who will guard their religion?"

•

[١٧٦] - وَقَالَ ابْنُ مَسْعُودٍ: إِذَا وَقَعَ النَّاسُ فِي الشَّرِّ فَقُلْ: «لَا أُسْوَةَ لِي فِي الشَّرِّ» لِيُوَطِّنْ المَرْءُ نَفْسَهُ عَلَى أَنَّهُ إِنْ كَفَرَ النَّاسُ كُلُّهُمْ لَمْ يَكْفُرْ.

176 — Ibn Mas'ūd said: "If the people fall into evil then you should say: 'I will not follow an evil example.' One should be acquainted with (the conviction that) that if all of the people (of the earth) disbelieve, then he will not."[1]

•

[١٧٧] - وَقَالَ عُمَرُ بْنُ الخَطَّابِ لِسُوَيْدِ بْنِ غَفَلَةَ: إِنَّكَ لَعَلَّكَ أَنْ تَخَلَّفَ بَعْدِي، فَأَطِعِ الأَمِيرَ وَإِنْ كَانَ عَبْدًا مُجَدَّعًا إِنْ ظَلَمَكَ فَاصْبِرْ وَإِنْ حَرَمَكَ فَاصْبِرْ وَإِنْ أَرَادَكَ عَلَى أَمْرٍ يَنْقُضُ دِينَكَ فَقُلْ دَمِي دُونَ دِينِي.

177 — 'Umar Ibn Al-Khaṭṭāb said to Suwaid Ibn Ghafalah[2] (d. 80H): "Perhaps you will live longer than me so (I advise you to) obey the leader even if he is a slave with amputated limbs, if he oppresses

---

1 — Collected by Aṭ-Ṭabarānī in *Al-Kabīr* (8640, 8641).

Benefit of the narration: The narration indicates that the believer should fortify himself with sufficient knowledge of the religion that will give him the type of conviction and firm-footedness, that will protect him from falling prey to being a blind follower in the affairs of his dīn. If he follows just for the sake of following, without his own knowledge-based resolution, then he will follow them into disbelief if they were to embark upon a path of kufr, and Allāh's aid is sought.

2 — He is Suwaid Ibn Ghafalah Ibn 'Awsajah Al-Ju'fī. He was alive during the period of Jāhiliyyah as a mature man and embraced Islām during the lifetime of the Prophet (ﷺ) but didn't meet him but arrived in Madīnah the day the Prophet passed away.

you then be patient, and if he prevents you (from something) then be patient, but if he wants you for something that opposes your dīn then say: *(Take) my blood but not my dīn!*"[1]

•

[١٧٨] - وَقَالَ مُطَرِّفُ بْنُ عَبْدِ اللَّهِ: مَنْ بَذَلَ دِينَهُ دُونَ مَالِهِ أَوْرَثَهُ اللَّهُ الفَقْرَ

وَحَشَرَهُ يَوْمَ الْقِيَامَةِ فِيمَنْ يَحْمِلُ الرَّايَةَ بَيْنَ يَدَيْ إِبْلِيسَ إِلَى جَهَنَّمَ.

178 — Mutarrif Ibn 'Abdullāh[2] (95H) said: "He who forfeits his dīn and not his wealth,[3] Allāh will make him inherit poverty and he will be raised on the Day of Judgement carrying a banner before Iblīs, heading for the fire."

•

[١٧٩] - وَقَالَ الْفُضَيْلُ بْنُ عِيَاضٍ: أَوْثَقُ عُرَى الإِسْلَامِ الْحُبُّ فِي اللَّهِ

وَالْبُغْضُ فِي اللَّهِ.

179 — Fudhail Ibn 'Iyādh said: "The strongest bond of Īmān is love for the sake of Allāh and hate for the sake of Allāh."[4]

•

---

1 — Collected by Nu'aym Ibn Hammād in *Al-Fitan* (389) and Al-Baihaqī in *Al-Ibānatul-Kubrā* (8/159) and Ibn Abī Shaibah in *Al-Musannaf* (6/544: 33711) and Ibn Zinjawayhi in *Al-Amwāl* (p.34) and Al-Khallāl in *As-Sunnah* (54).

2 — He is Mutarrif Ibn 'Abdillāh Ibn Shikhīr, Abū 'Abdillāh Al-'Āmiri.

3 — Such as one who is faced with losing his wealth or his religion, and he chooses to forfeit his religion over his wealth.

4 — Collected by Ibn Abī Shaibah in *Al-Īmān* (111) and Muhammad Ibn Nasr in *Ta'dhīm Qadrus-Salāh* (400).

Benefit of the narration: The narration indicates the great station of *Al-Walā' wal-Barā'* (allegiance and disavowal for the sake of Allāh). This important fundamental revolves around loving what Allāh loves, and hating what Allāh hates.

[١٨٠] - وَقَالَ الْفُضَيْلُ: صَاحِبُ بِدْعَةٍ لَا تَأْمَنْهُ عَلَى دِينِكَ وَلَا تُشَاوِرْهُ فِي أَمْرِكَ وَلَا تَجْلِسْ إِلَيْهِ فَإِنَّهُ مَنْ جَلَسَ إِلَى صَاحِبِ بِدْعَةٍ وَرَّثَهُ اللَّهُ اَلْعَمَى.

180 — Fudhail said: "Do not trust the person of innovation with your religion, do not consult with him in your affairs, nor sit with him, for the one who sits with him will inherit blindness (of the heart)."[1]

•

[١٨١] - وَقَالَ الْفُضَيْلُ: نَظَرُ اَلْمُؤْمِنِ إِلَى الْمُؤْمِنِ جَلَاءُ الْقَلْبِ وَنَظَرُ الرَّجُلِ إِلَى صَاحِبِ الْبِدْعَةِ يُوَرِّثُهُ الْعَمَى يَعْنِى فِي قَلْبِهِ.

181 — Fudhail said: "The look of one believer to another causes illumination of the heart, while the look of a believer towards the person of innovation, brings about blindness (of the heart)."[2]

•

[١٨٢] - وَكَانَ الْفُضَيْلُ يَقُولُ: أُسْلُكْ حَيَاةَ طَيِّبَةَ الْإِسْلَامَ وَالسُّنَّةَ.

182 — Fudhail used to say: "Take the path of a good life; (that of) Islām and the Sunnah."[3]

•

[١٨٣] - وَقَالَ مُجَاهِدٌ فِي قَوْلِ اللَّهِ - عَزَّ وَجَلَّ - {فَلَنُحْيِيَنَّهُ حَيَاةً طَيِّبَةً} قَالَ: «حُسْنَ الرَّأْيِ يَعْنِى السُّنَّةَ.»

---

1 — Collected by Ibn Battah in Al-Ibānatul-Kubrā (442) and Al-Lillakā'ī (264).

2 — Collected by Abū Nu'aym in Al-Hilyah (8/103) and Abū Tāhir As-Silafī in At-Tuyūriyāt (280). See footnote under narration 121.

3 — Collected by Abū Nu'aym in Al-Hilyah (8/99).

Benefit of the narration: The narration and the two that follow, indicates that a good life revolves around following Islām with the correct understanding of the Sunnah.

183 — Mujāhid used to say in relation to the verse; *"...then we shall cause him to live a good life..."*[1] He said: "[It means] cause him to hold good correct opinions — i.e. (in accordance to) the Sunnah."

•

[١٨٤] - وَقَالَ الْفُضَيْلُ: طُوبَى لِمَنْ مَاتَ عَلَى الْإِسْلَامِ وَالسُّنَّةِ، ثُمَّ بَكَى الْفُضَيْلُ عَلَى زَمَانٍ تَظْهَرُ فِيهِ الْبِدْعَةُ، فَإِذَا كَانَ ذَلِكَ فَأَكْثِرُوا مِنْ قَوْلِ مَا شَاءَ اللَّهُ»

184 — Fudhail said: "Glad tidings to he who dies upon Islām and the Sunnah." Then Fudhail cried about the period wherein innovations became manifest (then said) "If his affair is such (i.e. upon Islām and the Sunnah) then let them be plentiful in saying *'Māshā'Allāh!'"*[2]

•

[١٨٥] - وَقَالَ الْفُضَيْلُ: مَنْ جَلَسَ مَعَ صَاحِبِ بِدْعَةٍ لَمْ يُعْطَ الْحِكْمَةَ.

185 — Fudhail said: "Whoever sits with a person of innovation has not been given wisdom."[3]

•

1 — Surāh An-Nahl (16): 97

2 — Collected by Al-Lillakā'ī (268) and Al-Baihaqī in *Ash-Shu'ab* (9474).

3 — Collected by Al-Baihaqī in *Ash-Shu'ab* (9482) Al-Lillakā'ī (1149) and Abū Nu'aym in *Al-Hilyah* (8/103).

Benefit of the narration: When wisdom is mentioned in the book of Allāh it refers to the Sunnah, as the scholars of Tafsīr state. Thus the one who sits with the people who bring about a substitute to this Qur'anic 'wisdom' and espouses its opposite, finding no problem sitting with them, with the knowledge that the Sunnah itself warns against this, then this action of his is diametrically opposed to the very wisdom he claims to be following. It is therefore fair to say that he has not been given the wisdom he presumes he is upon.

[١٨٦] - وَقَالَ الْفُضَيْلُ: لَا تَجْلِسْ مَعَ صَاحِبٍ بِدْعَةٍ فَإِنِّي أَخْشَى عَلَيْكَ اللَّعْنَةَ.

186 — Fudhail said: "Do not sit with a person of innovation for indeed I fear for you the curse (of Allāh)."[1]

•

[١٨٧] - وَقَالَ الْفُضَيْلُ: مَنْ وَقَّرَ صَاحِبَ بِدْعَةٍ فَقَدْ أَعَانَ عَلَى هَدْمِ الإِسْلَامِ.

187 — Fudhail said: "Whoever facilitates ease for a person of innovation has aided in the destruction of Islām."[2]

•

[١٨٨] - وَقَالَ الْفُضَيْلُ: إِنَّ لِلَّهِ عِبَادًا تَحْيَا بِهِمُ الْبِلَادُ وَهُمْ أَصْحَابُ السُّنَّةِ مَنْ كَانَ مِنْهُمْ يَعْقِلُ مَا يَدْخُلُ جَوْفَهُ وَمَنْ كَانَ كَذَلِكَ كَانَ فِي حِزْبِ اللَّهِ - عَزَّ وَجَلَّ.

188 — Fudhail said: "Indeed Allāh has servants who, by way of them, He gives life to the land! They are the companions of the

---

1 — Collected by Al-Baihaqī in *Ash-Shu'ab* (9472) Al-Lillakā'ī (262).

Benefit of the narration: The Prophet (ﷺ) said, "Al-Madīnah is a sanctity from (Mount) 'Ayr to (Mount) Thowr, whosoever brings about an innovation in it, or accommodates an innovator, then upon him is the curse of Allāh and the curse of those who curse and the angels and all of the people. No form of repentance will be accepted from him nor ransom." Collected by Abū Dāwūd (4530) and An-Nasā'ī (6911, 6912) and At-Tirmidhī (2127) and declared 'sahīh' by Al-Albānī in *Al-Irwā'* (1058). That which Fudhail Ibn 'Iyādh feared is what was mentioned by the Prophet here.

2 — Collected by Al-Lillakā'ī (273) from the statement of Ibrāhīm Ibn Maysarah. Shaikhul-Islām Ibn Taimiyah said: "This statement is well known from the statement of Fudhail Ibn 'Iyādh." [*Majmū'ul Fatāwā* (18/346)]

Benefit of the narration: The appearance of innovation has been the primary cause of the weakening of this Ummah. For certainly, Islam is the Sunnah and the Sunnah is Islam. Thus when the Muslims stray from the Sunnah they stray from the cause of their success. Therefore aiding the innovator is in essence aiding the destruction of the religion.

Sunnah: whosoever is from them, then he is aware of what he puts inside himself. Whosoever is like this, then he is from the party of Allāh (عَزَّوَجَلَّ)."

•

[١٨٩] - وَقَالَ الْفُضَيْلُ: مَنْ تَبِعَ جِنَازَةَ مُبْتَدِعٍ لَمْ يَزَلْ فِي سُخْطِ اللَّهِ حَتَّى يَرْجِعَ.

189 — Fudhail said: "Whosoever follows the funeral procession of the innovator does not cease to be in the anger of Allāh until he returns."[1]

•

[١٩٠] - وَقَالَ سُفْيَانُ بْنُ عُيَيْنَةَ لِرَجُلٍ: مِنْ أَيْنَ جِئْتَ قَالَ: مِنْ جِنَازَةِ فُلَانِ بْنِ فُلَانٍ قَالَ: لَا حَدَّثْتُكَ بِحَدِيثٍ اِسْتَغْفِرِ اللَّهَ وَلَا تَعُدْ، نَظَرْتَ إِلَى رَجُلٍ يُبْغِضُ أَصْحَابَ رَسُولِ اللَّهِ - صلى الله عليه وسلم - فَاتَّبَعْتَ جِنَازَتَهُ

190 — Sufyān Ibn ʿUyainah[2] (198H) said to a man: "Where have you come from?"

He responded: "From the Janāzah of such and such, the son of such and such."

So he said: "I will not narrate a (single) hadīth to you! Seek the forgiveness of Allāh and do not repeat this! You see a man hating

---

1 — Al-Harawī collects it from the statement of Sufyān Ibn ʿUyainah (953)

Benefit of the narration: When innovation in the religion causes the destruction of the religion, there is no doubt therefore, that it brings about the anger of Allāh. The pious predecessors hated that the innovator be shown honour and respect since this is his reality. From the wisdoms of the funeral procession is honouring the deceased, this statement therefore (as is the case with the following two narrations), revolves around preventing the means to raising the station of innovations and the innovator.

2 — He is Sufyān Ibn ʿUyainah Ibn Abī ʿImrān Maimūn Al-Hilālī, Abū Muhammad Al-Kūfī.

the companions of the Messenger of Allāh (ﷺ) and you follow his funeral?!"[1]

•

[١٩١] - وَقَالَ هَارُونُ بْنُ زِيَادٍ: سَمِعْتُ الْفِرْيَابِيَّ وَرَجُلٌ يَسْأَلُهُ عَنْ مَنْ شَتَمَ أَبَا

بَكْرٍ، قَالَ كَافِرٌ، قَالَ فَنُصَلِّي عَلَيْهِ قَالَ لَا، فَسَأَلْتُهُ كَيْفَ نَصْنَعُ بِهِ وَهُوَ يَقُولُ

لَا إِلَهَ إِلَّا اَللَّهُ قَالَ لَا تَمَسُّوهُ بِأَيْدِيكُمْ اِدْفَعُوهُ بِالْخَشَبِ حَتَّى تُوَارُوهُ فِي حُفْرَتِهِ.

191 — Hārūn Ibn Ziyād said: "I heard Al-Firyābī[2] (212H), when a man asked him about a man who curses Abū Bakr, say: *"He is a Kāfir!"* So he (the questioner) said: *"So should we pray over him?"* He said: *"No!"* So he said: *"Then what should we do with him since he says: 'Lā ilāha illallāh'?"*[3] He said: *"Don't touch him with your hands! Push him with some wood until he enters his hole."*[4]

•

[١٩٢] - وَقَالَ مُحَمَّدُ بْنُ بَشَّارٍ قُلْتُ لِعَبْدِ الرَّحْمَنِ بْنِ مَهْدِيٍّ: أَحْضُرُ جِنَازَةَ

مَنْ سَبَّ أَصْحَابَ رَسُولِ اللَّهِ - صلى الله عليه وسلم - فَقَالَ: لَوْ كَانَ مِنْ

عَصَبَتِي مَا وَرَّثْتُهُ.

---

1 — Collected by Al-Lillakā'ī (2816).

2 — He is Muhammad Ibn Yūsuf Ibn Wāqid Adh-Dhabi Al-Firyābī.

3 — i.e. he was a Muslim.

4 — Collected by Al-Khallāl in *As-Sunnah* (794).

Benefit of the narration: The narration indicates that the Salaf made every effort to instill hatred for innovation in the hearts of their students and followers. Narrations of this sort make that point clear. There is no doubt the janazah is performed for the people of innovation in the normal way, but the person of Sunnah refrains from those funerals wherever possible, since following the janaazah is from enobling and showing respect to the deceased. This respect is not shown to one who disrespects the dīn of Allāh. Thus we see that the Salaf nurtured their followers upon this understanding.

192 — Muhammad Ibn Bashār[1] (252H) said: "I said to ʿAbdur-Rahmān Ibn Mahdī[2] (298H): 'Should I attend the funeral of one who curses the companions of the Messenger of Allāh?'

He responded: 'Even if he was from my relatives I would not inherit from him!'"[3]

•

[١٩٣] - وَقَالَ أَبُو بَكْرِ بْنُ عَيَّاشٍ لَا أُصَلِّي عَلَى رَافِضِيٍّ وَلَا حَرُورِيٍّ لِأَنَّ

الرَّافِضِيَّ يَجْعَلُ عُمَرَ كَافِرًا وَالْحَرُورِيَّ يَجْعَلُ عَلِيًّا كَافِرًا.

193 — Abū Bakr Ibn ʿAyyāsh[4] (d. 194H) said: "I would not pray over a Rāfidhi nor a Harūri (Kharijite) because the Rāfidhi declares ʿUmar a kāfir, while the Harūri makes ʿAlī a kāfir!"[5]

•

[١٩٤] - وَقَالَ طَلْحَةُ بْنُ مُصَرِّفٍ: الرَّافِضَةُ لَا تُنْكَحُ نِسَاؤُهُمْ وَلَا تُؤْكَلُ

ذَبَائِحُهُمْ لِأَنَّهُمْ أَهْلُ رِدَّةٍ.

194 — Talha Ibn Musarrif[6] (112H or later) said: "The women of the Rāfidhah are not to be married, neither is their slaughtered meat to be eaten, because they are apostates."[7]

---

1 — He is Muhammad Ibn Bashār Ibn ʿUthmān Al-ʿAbdi Al-Basri.

2 — He is ʿAbdur-Rahmān Ibn Mahdī Ibn Hassān Al-ʿAmbarī, Abū Saʿīd Al-Basrī. ʿAlī Ibn Al-Madīnī said: 'I have seen no one more knowledgeable than him."

3 — Benefit of the narration: This narration and those that follow, discuss the Rāfidhah who are deemed by the great imāms to be outside of the fold of Islām due to their heretic beliefs.

4 — He is Abū Bakr Ibn ʿAyyāsh Ibn Sālim Al-Asadī Al-Muqrī. He is well known by way of his kunya (i.e. Abū Bakr), and what is most correct is that is also his first name.

5 — Ibn Qudāma mentions the narration in *Al-Mughnī* (2/219).

6 — He is Talhah Ibn Musarrif Ibn ʿAmr Ibn Kaʿb Al-Yāmī.

7 — Al-Lillakāʾī collects upon the authority of Ahmad Ibn Yūnus the statement: "I do not eat the slaughtered meat of a man who is Rāfidhi, for as far as I am concerned, he is

[١٩٥] - وَقِيلَ لِلْحَسَنِ: إِنَّ فُلَانَا غَسَّلَ رَجُلاً مِنْ أَهْلِ الأَهْوَاءِ فَقَالَ عَرِّفُوهُ أَنَّهُ إِنْ مَاتَ لَمْ نُصَلِّ عَلَيْهِ.

195 — It was said to Hasan: "Indeed such and such washed a person from the people of desires." So he (Hasan) said: "Acquaint him with the fact that when he dies, we will not pray over him!"[1]

•

[١٩٦] - وَنَظَرَ ابْنُ سِيرِينَ إِلَى رَجُلٍ مِنْ أَصْحَابِهِ فِي بَعْضِ مَحَالِّ البَصْرَةِ فَقَالَ لَهُ: يَا فُلَانُ مَا تَصْنَعُ هَا هُنَا فَقَالَ عُدْتُ فُلَانًا مِنْ عِلَّةٍ، يَعْنِي رَجُلاً مِنْ أَهْلِ الأَهْوَاءِ فَقَالَ لَهُ ابْنُ سِيرِينَ: إِنْ مَرِضْتَ لَمْ نَعُدْكَ وَإِنْ مُتَّ لَمْ نُصَلِّ عَلَيْكَ إِلَّا أَنْ تَتُوبَ قَالَ تُبْتُ.

196 — Ibn Sīrīn saw a man from his companions in one of the pathways of Basra, so he said to him: *"Oh such and such what are you doing here?"* So he said: *"I came to visit such and such, (who was a person of desires,) who was ill"*, so he (Ibn Sīrīn) said to him: *"If you are ill, we will not visit you, and if you die we will not pray over you, unless you repent!"* So he said: *"I repent! I repent!"*

•

[١٩٧] - وَقَالَ الْفُضَيْلُ: آكُلُ طَعَامَ الْيَهُودِيِّ وَالنَّصْرَانِيِّ وَلَا آكُلُ طَعَامَ صَاحِبِ بِدْعَةٍ.

---

an apostate."

1 — Ibn Battah mentions in *Al-Ibānatul-Kubrā* (525) on the authority of Ayyūb As-Sikhtiyānī that he was called to wash a deceased individual. So he went with the people and when the face of the deceased was uncovered he knew him so he said (to those present): "Come to your companion, for indeed I will not wash him, I saw him walking with a person of innovation."

197 — Fudhail said: "I would eat the food of the Jews and the Christians, but I will not eat the food of a person of innovation."[1]

•

[١٩٨] - وَكَانَ يَقُولُ: اللَّهُمَّ لَا تَجْعَلْ لِصَاحِبِ بِدْعَةٍ عِنْدِي يَدًا فَيُحِبَّهُ قَلْبِي.

198 — He (Fudhail) used to say: "Oh Allāh! Do not let a person of bid'ah have a hand over me, and thus let my heart love him."[2]

•

[١٩٩] - قَالَ الْفُضَيْلُ: إِذَا عَلِمَ اللَّهُ مِنْ رَجُلٍ أَنَّهُ مُبْغِضٌ لِصَاحِبِ بِدْعَةٍ رَجَوْتُ أَنْ يَغْفِرَ اللَّهُ لَهُ وَإِنْ قَلَّ عَمَلُهُ.

199 — Fudhail said: "If Allāh knows from a man that he hates the people of desires, then I hope that Allāh will forgive his sins (due to this) even if his actions are little."[3/4]

•

[٢٠٠] - وَقَالَ: الْمَرْوَزِيُّ: سَأَلْتُ أَبَا عَبْدِ اللَّهِ عَمَّنْ شَتَمَ أَبَا بَكْرٍ وَعُمَرَ وَعُثْمَانَ وَعَائِشَةَ رَضِيَ اللَّهُ عَنْهُمْ فَقَالَ: مَا أَرَاهُ عَلَى الإِسْلَامِ.

200 — Al-Marwazī said: "I asked Abū 'Abdullāh (Imām Ahmad) about one who curses Abū Bakr, 'Umar, 'Uthmān and 'Ā'ishah (رَضِيَ ٱللَّهُ عَنْهُمْ) so he said: 'I don't consider him upon Islām.'"[5]

•

1 — Collected by Al-Lillakā'ī (1149) and Abū Nu'aym in *Al-Hilyah* (8/103).

2 — Collected by Al-Lillakā'ī (275).

3 — Since hatred for bid'ah is an evidence that one loves the Sunnah.

4 — Collected by Abū Nu'aym in *Al-Hilyah* (8/103) and As-Silafi in *At-Tuyūriyāt* (438) and Ibn 'Asākir in *Tārīkh Dimashq* (8/103).

5 — Collected by Al-Khallāl in *As-Sunnah* (782).

[٢٠١] - وَقَالَ مَالِكُ بنُ أَنَسٍ: الَّذِي يَشْتُمُ أَصْحَابَ رَسُولِ اللَّهِ (ﷺ)
لَيْسَ لَهُ سَهْمٌ - أَوْ قَالَ: نَصِيْبٌ فِي الإِسْلاَمِ.

201 — Imām Mālik said: "Whoever curses the companions of the
Messenger of Allāh (ﷺ) he has no lot (or he said: "He has
no portion...") of Islām."[1]

•

[٢٠٢] - وَقَالَ بِشْرُ بْنُ الْحَارِثِ: مَنْ شَتَمَ أَصْحَابَ رَسُولِ اللَّهِ - صَلَّى اللَّهُ
عَلَيْهِ وَسَلَّمَ - فَهُوَ كَافِرٌ وَإِنْ صَامَ وَصَلَّى وَزَعَمَ أَنَّهُ مِنَ الْمُسْلِمِينَ.

202 — Bishr Ibnil-Hārith[2] (227H) said: "Whoever curses the
companions of the Messenger of Allāh (ﷺ) then he is a
Kāfir, even if he fasts and prays and claims he is from the Muslims."

•

[٢٠٣] - وَقَالَ الأَوْزَاعِيُّ: مَنْ شَتَمَ أَبَا بَكْرٍ الصِّدِّيقَ رَضِيَ اللَّهُ عَنْهُ فَقَدْ ارْتَدَّ
عَنْ دِينِهِ وَأَبَاحَ دَمَهُ.

---

1 — Collected by Al-Khallāl in *As-Sunnah* (779). Imām Khallāl also collects (760)
the statement of Imām Mālik when it was mentioned to him that a man speaks ill
of and disparages (the companions of the Prophet) so he recited (the Quranic verse):
"Muhammad (ﷺ) is the Messenger of Allāh, and those who are with him are
severe against disbelievers, and merciful among themselves. You see them bowing and
falling down prostrate (in prayer), seeking Bounty from Allāh and (His) Good Pleasure.
The mark of them (i.e. of their Faith) is on their faces (foreheads) from the traces of
(their) prostration (during prayers). This is their description in the *Taurāt* (Torah). But
their description in the *Injīl* (Gospel) is like a (sown) seed which sends forth its shoot,
then makes it strong, it then becomes thick, and it stands straight on its stem, delighting
the sowers so that Allāh may enrage by them the disbelievers."
Imām Mālik (then said): "Whosoever finds in his heart rage for the companions (of the
Prophet), then the verse applies to him!"

2 — He is Bishr Ibn Al-Hārith Al-Marwazī (also known as Bishr Al-Hāfī) Abū Nasr.

203 — Al-Auzā'ī[1] (157H) said: "Whoever curses Abū Bakr As-Siddīq — May Allāh be pleased with him — then he has apostatized from his dīn, and he has made his blood permissible."

●

[٢٠٤] - وَقَالَ أَبُو عُبَيْدٍ القَاسِمُ بْنُ سَلَّامٍ: لَا حَظَّ لِلرَّافِضِيِّ فِي اَلْفَيْءِ وَالْغَنِيمَةِ لِقَوْلِ اللَّهِ - عَزَّ وَجَلَّ - {وَاَلَّذِينَ جَاءُوا مِنْ بَعْدِهِمْ يَقُولُونَ} اَلْآيَةَ.

204 — Abū 'Ubaid Al-Qāsim Ibn Sallām[2] (224H) said: "The Rāfidhah have no portion of *fay'*[3] and the spoils of war due to the statement of Allāh: *'And those who come after them they say...'*"[4]

●

[٢٠٥] - وَقَالَ حَمَّادُ بْنُ زَيْدٍ كُنْتُ مَعَ أَيُّوبَ وَيُونُسَ وَابْنِ عَوْنٍ فَمَرَّ بِهِمْ عَمْرُو بْنُ عُبَيْدٍ فَسَلَّمَ عَلَيْهِمْ وَوَقَفَ فَلَمْ يَرُدُّوا عَلَيْهِ ثُمَّ جَازَ، فَمَا ذَكَرُوهُ.

205 — Hammād Ibn Zaid said: "I was with Ayyūb (As-Sikhtiyānī), Yūnus (Ibn 'Ubaid) and ('Abdullāh) Ibn 'Aun when 'Amr Ibn 'Ubaid passed by them and gave salām, then stopped. None of them responded to him, so he continued and they didn't (even) mention him (thereafter)."[5]

---

1 — He is 'Abdur-Rahmān Ibn 'Amr Ibn Abī 'Amr Al-Auzā'ī.

2 — He is Abū 'Ubaid Al-Qāsim Ibn Sallām Al-Baghdādi Al-Harawī.

3 — The difference between the *fay'* and *ghanīmah* is that: while they are both considered spoils of war, *fay'* is a reference to spoils of war obtained without fighting (i.e. when the enemy flee without battle), while *ghanīmah* is spoils of war obtained after being victorious after battle.

4 — Collected by Al-Khallāl in *As-Sunnah* (792). The completion of the verse is *"they say: 'O our lord forgive us and our brothers who have preceded us in Īmān...'"* (Suratul Hashr (9):59) — indicating the fact that the Rāfidhah have no portion of the verse, since they curse those who have preceded them, and at the head of those they curse are the Sahābah (may Allāh be pleased with them all).

5 — Collected by 'Abdullāh Ibn Ahmad in *As-Sunnah* (2/435) and Ibn Battah in *Al-Ibānatul-Kubrā* (1964).

[٢٠٦] - وَقَالَ الْفُضَيْلُ: يَدُ اللَّهِ عَلَى الْجَمَاعَةِ وَلَا يَنْظُرُ اللَّهُ إِلَى صَاحِبِ بِدْعَةٍ.

206 Fudhail (Ibn 'Iyādh) said: "The hand of Allāh is upon the Jamā'ah, and Allāh doesn't look at the person of innovation!"

•

[٢٠٧] - وَقَالَ زَائِدَةُ قُلْتُ لِمَنْصُورٍ يَا أَبَا عَتَّابٍ! الْيَوْمُ الَّذِي يَصُومُ فِيهِ أَحَدُنَا يُنْتَقَصُ فِيهِ الَّذِينَ يَنْتَقِصُونَ أَبَا بَكْرٍ وَعُمَرَ رَضِيَ اللَّهُ عَنْهُمَا قَالَ نَعَمْ.

207 — Zā'idah (Ibn Qudāmah)[1] (160H) said, "I said to Mansūr:[2] 'Oh Abū 'Attāb! On the day that one of us fasts may he disparage those who dispraise Abū Bakr and 'Umar?' He said: 'Na'am! (Yes!).'"[3]

•

[٢٠٨] - وَكَانَ الْحَسَنُ يَقُولُ: لَيْسَ لِأَصْحَابِ الْبِدْعَةِ غِيبَةٌ.

---

1 — He is Zā'idah Ibn Qudāmah Ath-Thaqafī, Abū Salt Al-Kūfī. He only ever narrated from the people of Sunnah. Ahmad Ibn Yūsuf mentions: "I saw Zuhair Ibn Mu'āwiyah approach Zā'idah and he addressed him concerning an individual that he was narrating hadīth to. So he said: 'Is he from the people of Sunnah?' So he responded: 'I don't know him to be upon innovation.' So he responded: 'How preposterous! Is he from the people of Sunnah?!' So Zuhair said to him: 'When did the people become like this?!' (i.e. Cross questioning concerning the state of people.) So Zā'idah responded: 'When did the people start cursing Abū Bakr and Umar?!'" Collected by Khatībul-Baghdādī in Al-Jāmi' Li Akhlāqir-Rāwī (748).

2 — He is Mansūr Ibn Mu'tamir (d. 123H).

3 — Collected by Al-Khallāl (789) and Abū Nu'aym in Al-Hilyah (5/41). This position is based in the fact that they did not consider disparaging the people of innovation backbiting.

208 — Al-Hasan (Al-Basrī) used to say: "There is no *ghībah* (backbiting) for the person of innovation." (i.e. dispraising him is not considered *ghībah*).[1]

•

[٢٠٩] - وَقَالَ عَطَاءٌ: مَا أَذِنَ اللَّهُ لِصَاحِبِ بِدْعَةٍ فِي تَوْبَةٍ.

209 — 'Atā' said: "Allāh has not permitted a person of innovation to make *taubah*."[2]

•

[٢١٠] - وَقَالَ أَبُو عُبَيْدٍ: عَاشَرْتُ النَّاسَ وَكَلَّمْتُ أَهْلَ الكَلَامِ فَمَا رَأَيْتُ قَوْمًا أَوْسَخَ وَسَخًا وَلَا أَقْذَرَ قَذَرًا وَلَا أَضْعَفَ حُجَّةً وَلَا أَحْمَقَ مِنَ الرَّافِضَةِ.

210 — Abū 'Ubaid said: "I have experienced (various) people and I have not seen a people filthier, nor more disgusting, nor weaker in establishing evidence or more foolish than the Rāfidhah."[3]

•

[٢١١] - وَذَكَرْتُ الأَهْوَاءَ عِنْدَ رَقَبَةَ بْنِ مِصْقَلَةَ، فَقَالَ: أَمَّا الرَّافِضَةُ فَإِنَّهُمْ اتَّخَذُوا البُهْتَانَ حُجَّةً وَأَمَّا المُرْجِئَةُ فَعَلَى دِينِ المُلُوكِ وَأَمَّا الزَّيْدِيَّةُ فَأَحْسَبُ أَنَّ الَّذِي وَضَعَ لَهُمْ رَأْيَهُمْ اِمْرَأَةٌ وَأَمَّا المُعْتَزِلَةُ فَوَاللَّهِ مَا خَرَجْتُ إِلَى ضَيْعَتِي فَظَنَنْتُ أَنِّي أَرْجِعُ إِلَّا وَهُمْ قَدْ رَجَعُوا عَنْ رَأْيِهِمْ.

---

1 — Collected by Al-Lillakā'ī (278, 279, 280) and Khatīb Al-Baghdādī in *Al-Kifāyah* (p.430) and Al-Baihaqī in *Ash-Shu'ab* (6793, 9675).

2 — Collected by Al-Lillakā'ī (283) and Abū Nu'aym in *Al-Hilyah* (5/198).

3 — Collected by Ad-Dūrī in Tārīkh Ibn Ma'īn (4992) and Al-Khallāl in *As-Sunnah* (795) and Ibn 'Asākir in *Tārīkh Dimashq* (49/80).

211 — I mentioned the affair of desires to Raqabah Ibn Masqalah[1] (129H) and he said: "As for the Rāfidhah then they have taken to using falsehood as evidence, and as for the Murji'ah then they are upon the religion of the kings (i.e. they appease the kings and appeal to the sinful ones from them, due to the fact that they hold that sins do not affect ones īmān).

As for the Zaidiyah,[2] then I believe the one who created their opinion was a woman, and as for the Mu'tazilah, then by Allāh, I did not leave out upon one of my chores except that I expected to return and find that they have changed their opinion!"

•

[٢١٢] - وَقَالَ طَلْحَةُ بْنُ مُصَرِّفٍ: لَوْلَا أَنِّي عَلَى وُضُوءٍ لَأَخْبَرْتُكُمْ بِمَا تَقُولُ الرَّافِضَةُ.

212 — Talha Ibn Musarrif said: "If it were not for the fact that I am in the state of wudhū', I would mention to you what the Rāfidhah say!"[3]

•

[٢١٣] - وَقَالَ مُغِيرَةُ: خَرَجَ جَرِيرُ بْنُ عَبْدِ اللَّهِ وَعَدِيُّ بْنُ حَاتِمٍ وَحَنْظَلَةُ الْكَاتِبُ مِنَ الْكُوفَةِ حَتَّى نَزَلُوا قَرْقِيسِيَاء وَقَالُوا لَا نُقِيمُ بِبَلْدَةٍ يُشْتَمُ فِيهَا عُثْمَانُ بْنُ عَفَّانَ.

---

1 — He is Raqabah Ibn Masqalah, Abū 'Abdillāh Al-'Abdī Al-Kūfī.

2 — One of the lightest sects of the Shi'ah in terms of deviation.

3 — Collected by Abū Nu'aym in *Al-Hilyah* (5/15) and Al-Lillakā'ī (2401).

213 — Mughīrah said: "I was with Jarīr Ibn 'Abdillāh[1] (d. 51H) and 'Adiyy Ibn Hātim[2] (d. 68H) and Handhalah[3] the scribe (died shortly after the death of 'Alī (رَضِيَاللّهُعَنهُ), from Kūfah, when they passed by Qarqisiyā' (a township close to the river Euphrates) and they said: 'We will not take up residence in a place that curses 'Uthmān Ibn 'Affān.'"[4]

•

[٢١٤] - وَقَالَ أَحْمَدُ بْنُ عَبْدِ اللّٰهِ بْنِ يُونُسَ بَاعَ مُحَمَّدُ بْنُ عَبْدِ العَزِيزِ التَّيْمِيُّ

دَارَهُ وَقَالَ: لَا أُقِيمُ بِالْكُوفَةِ بَلْدَةٍ يُشْتَمُ فِيهَا أَصْحَابُ رَسُولِ اللّٰهِ (صَلَّىاللّهُعَلَيهِوَسَلَّمَ).

214 — Ahmad Ibn 'Abdullāh Ibn Yūnus[5] (227H) said: "Muhammad Ibn 'Abdil-'Azīz At-Taymī sold his house and said: 'I will not remain in Kūfah, a land wherein the companions of the Messenger of Allāh are cursed!'"[6]

---

1 — He is Jarīr Ibn 'Abdullāh Al-Bajali, the famous companion of the Prophet (عَلَيْهِالسَّلَامُ).

2 — He is 'Adiyy Ibn Hātim At-Tā'i, the famous companion of the Prophet (عَلَيْهِالسَّلَامُ).

3 — He is Handhalah Ibnir-Rabī' At-Tamīmī, the well-known companion of the Prophet, popularly known as Handhalah Al-Kātib or Handhalah the Scribe

4 — Collected by Al-Bukhārī in Al-Tārīkhul-Kabīr (3/36) and At-Tabarāni in Al-Mu'jamul-Kabīr (2/293/2217) and Al-Lillakā'ī (2371). Al-Hāfidh Ibn Hajr mentions in the biography of Jarīr and Handhalah in his book Al-Isābah (1/475) and 2/134) that they refrained from involvement in the turmoil that occurred after the death of the Prophet, they left Kūfah and travelled to Qarsīsiyah, and both died there. Ibn 'Abdil-Hakam mentions in Al-Jāmi' (145) the statement of Imām Mālik: "It is not befitting to take up residence in a land that other than the truth is acted upon and wherein the Salaf are cursed." He then mentions as an evidence for that the affair of Abud-Dardā, when he was opposed with opinion in opposition to the Sunnah (he had presented): "I will not take up residence in a land you are in!" — and he left! Imām Mālik then said: "They used to leave due to words, while this individual remains (in a place wherein) other than the truth is acted upon, and where the Salaf are disparaged! Even though Allāh says: '(He who migrates (from his home) in the cause of Allāh,) He will find on earth many dwelling places and plenty to live by...'" Sūratun-Nisā' (4): 100

5 — He is Ahmad Ibn 'Abdullāh Ibn Yūnus At-Taimi Al-Yarbū'i Abū 'Abdillāh Al-Kūfī.

6 — Collected by Ibn Abī Hātim in Al-Jarhu Wat-Ta'dīl (8/6) and Tārīkh Ibn Ma'īn (Riwayatud-Dūri: 814)

[٢١٥] - وَقَالَ العَوَّامُ بْنُ حَوْشَبٍ: أَدْرَكْتُ مَنْ أَدْرَكْتُ مِنْ صَدْرِ هَذِهِ الأُمَّةِ

بَعْضُهُمْ يَقُولُ لِبَعْضٍ: أَذْكُرُوا مَحَاسِنَ أَصْحَابِ رَسُولِ اللَّهِ ﷺ لِتَأْتَلِفَ

عَلَيْهِ القُلُوبُ وَلَا تَذْكُرُوا مَا شَجَرَ بَيْنَهُمْ فَتُحَرِّشُوا النَّاسَ عَلَيْهِمْ.

215 — Al-ʿAwwām Ibn Hawshab[1] (148H) said: "I met those whom
I have met from the first generation of this Ummah, they would say
to each other: 'Mention the good points concerning the companions
of the Messenger of Allāh that the hearts may be united upon that,
and do not mention the disputes that occurred between them and
thus the hearts split over them.'"[2]

•

[٢١٦] - وَقَالَ سُفْيَانُ بْنُ عُيَيْنَةَ: لَا يُغَلُّ قَلْبُ أَحَدٍ عَلَى أَحَدٍ مِنْ أَصْحَابِ

رَسُولِ اللَّهِ - (ﷺ) - إِلَّا كَانَ قَلْبُهُ عَلَى المُسْلِمِينَ أَغَلَّ.

216 — Sufyān Ibn ʿUyainah said: "No one's heart has malice and
rancour for any of the companions of the Messenger of Allāh, except
that their hearts are greater in harbouring rancour and malice for
the Muslims (in general)."

•

[٢١٧] - وَقَالَ سُفْيَانُ (فِي قَوْلِهِ تَعَالَى) {تِلْكَ أُمَّةٌ قَدْ خَلَتْ لَهَا مَا كَسَبَتْ

وَلَكُمْ مَا كَسَبْتُمْ} وَقَالَ أَصْحَابُ مُحَمَّدٍ - (ﷺ).

---

1 — He is Al-ʿAwām Ibn Hawshab Ibn Yazīd Ash-Shaibānī, Abū ʿĪsā Al-Wāsitī.

2 — Collected by Al-Khallāl in As-Sunnah (829) and As-Sunnah of Harb Al-Kirmānī
(466) and Al-Ājjurī in Ash-Shariʿah (1891) and Al-Khatīb in Al-Jāmiʿ (1359).

Benefit of the narration: The narration indicates that the Salaf of this Ummah used
to nurture their students and followers upon understanding that the sahabah are to be
praised and mentioned only with good. Since they were the carriers of the Qurʾān and
Sunnah. This point is made in all of the well-known books of creed.

217 — Sufyān said concerning the statement of Allāh: *'That is a nation that has passed for it is what it has earned and to you is what you have earned'* [SŪRAH AL-BAQARAH (2):134] — he said: "The companions of Muhammad (صَلَّى اللّٰهُ عَلَيْهِ وَسَلَّمَ)."[1]

•

[٢١٨] - وَقَالَ الشَّعْبِيُّ: نَظَرْتُ فِي الأَهْوَاءِ وَكَلَّمْتُ أَهْلَهَا فَلَمْ أَرَ قَوْمًا أَقَلَّ عَقْلاً مِنْ اَلْخَشَبِيَّةِ.

218 — Ash-Sha'bī said: "I have looked into the affair of desires (i.e. innovations) and I have spoken to its people and I have not a people with less intellect than the Khashabiyyah."[2/3]

•

[٢١٩] - وَقَالَ عَاصِمُ بْنُ ضَمْرَةَ قُلْتُ: لِلْحَسَنِ بْنِ عَلِيٍّ إِنَّ الشِّيعَةَ يَزْعُمُونَ أَنَّ عَلِيًّا يَرْجِعُ فَقَالَ: كَذَبُوا لَوْ عَلِمْنَا ذَلِكَ مَا تَزَوَّجَ نِسَاؤُهُ وَلَا قَسَمْنَا مَالَهُ.

219 — 'Āsim Ibn Dhamrah[4] (174H) said: "I said to Al-Hasan Ibn 'Alī: *'The Shī'ah claim that 'Alī is going to return!'* He said: *'They have lied! If we knew of this then his wives would not have remarried neither would we have divided his estate.'*"[5]

•

---

1 — Abū Nu'aym collects in *Tabaqātul-Muhaddithīn* (2/110) the narration of 'Isām Ibn Yazīd who said: "I was sitting with Hamzah Azyāt and a man came and asked about the companions of Muhammad. He remained silent for a period then he recited the verse: *'That is a nation that has passed. For it is what it has earned, and to you is what you have earned.'*"

2 — The 'Khashabiyyah' was one of the names given to the Shi'ah Rāfidhah.

3 — Collected by 'Abdullāh Ibn Ahmad in *As-Sunnah* (1252) and Al-Khallāl in *As-Sunnah* (791) and Al-Lillakā'ī (2823).

4 — He is 'Āsim Ibn Dhamrah As-Salūlī Al-Kūfī.

5 — Collected by Al-Baghawī in *Musnad Ibnil-Ja'd* (2523) and 'Abdullāh Ibn Ahmad in *Zawā'id Fadhā'ilus-Sahābah* (1128).

[٢٢٠] - وَقَالَ سُفْيَانُ الثَّوْرِيُّ: مَنْ فَضَّلَ عَلِيًّا عَلَى أَبِي بَكْرٍ وَعُمَرَ فَقَدْ عَابَهُمَا
وَعَابَ مَنْ فَضَّلَهُ عَلَيْهِمَا.

220 — Sufyān Ath-Thawrī said: "Whosoever gives preference to
'Alī over Abū Bakr and 'Umar, then he has dispraised them, and he
has dispraised the one who he has preferred over them."[1/2]

•

[٢٢١] - وَقَالَ جَابِرُ بْنُ يَزِيدَ الْجُعْفِيُّ: قَالَ لِي مُحَمَّدُ بْنُ عَلِيٍّ: يَا جَابِرُ
بَلَغَنِي أَنَّ أَقْوَامًا بِالْعِرَاقِ يَتَنَاوَلُونَ أَبَا بَكْرٍ وَعُمَرَ وَيَزْعُمُونَ أَنَّهُمْ يُحِبُّونَنَا وَيَزْعُمُونَ
أَنِّي أَمَرْتُهُمْ بِذَلِكَ فَأَبْلِغْهُمْ أَنِّي إِلَى اللَّهِ مِنْهُمْ بَرِيءٌ وَالَّذِي نَفْسِي بِيَدِهِ لَوْ
وُلِّيتُ لَتَقَرَّبْتُ بِدِمَائِهِمْ إِلَى اللَّهِ - عز وجل - إِنَّ أَعْدَاءَ الإِسْلَام لَغَافِلُونَ عَنْهُمَا
بِقِلَّةِ حِرَاءٍ مَعَ رَسُولِ اللَّهِ (صَلَّى اللَّهُ عَلَيْهِ وَسَلَّمَ).

221 — Jābir Ibn Yazīd Al-Ju'fī[3] (127H or 132H) said: "Muhammad
Ibn 'Alī[4] (114H) said to me "Oh Jābir! It has reached me that a
people in Iraq speak ill of Abū Bakr and 'Umar! And they claim that
they love us! They (also) claim that I have commanded them with

---

1 — Meaning, whoever does so, has also dispraised 'Alī without even realising it,
because he claims that 'Alī remained silent, knowing he was better than Abū Bakr and
'Umar and this is a deficiency. While in actuality it is established that 'Alī ascended the
pulpit in Kūfah and said: *"The best of this Ummah after it Prophet is Abū Bakr and
'Umar"* collected by Ahmad (1/106) and Al-Lillakā'ī (2605) and Abū Nu'aym in *Al-Hilyah*
(7/199) and declared *'sahīh'* by Shaikh Al-Albānī in *Dhilālul-Jannah*. (p.472)

2 — Collected by Al-Lillakā'ī (2617) and Abū Nu'aym in *Al-Hilyah* (7/28).

3 — He is Jābir Ibn Yazīd Ibnil-Hārith Al-Ju'fī Al-Kūfī, He is a well-known narrator
that is abandoned in hadīth and was known to be a Shi'ite. Although the fact that
this narration is, in essence, a refutation of the Shītes from one of the offspring of 'Alī,
narrated by one who is himself a Shīte, then this may indicate the truthful nature of the
occurrence — *wallāhu-a'lam (and Allāh knows best)*.

4 — He is Muhammad Ibn 'Alī Ibnil-Husain Ibn 'Alī Ibn Abī Tālib Al-Hāshimī, the
great grandson of 'Alī Ibn Abī Tālib.

this! So inform them, that I free myself from them before Allāh, and by Him in whose hands is my soul, if I were to be placed in a position of authority, I would have drawn closer to Allāh with their blood,[1] for indeed these enemies of Islām are heedless regarding (the incident that occurred with) the two of them, alongside the Messenger (صَلَّىاللَّهُعَلَيْهِوَسَلَّمَ) upon the pinnacle of mount Hirā."[2/3]

•

[٢٢٢] - وقال جَابِرٌ: جَاءَ نَفَرٌ مِن النَّاسِ إِلَى عَلِيِّ بن الحُسَينِ، فَأَثْنَوا عَلَيهِ.

فَقَالَ: مَا أَكْذَبَكُمْ وَأَجْرَأَكُمْ عَلَى اللَّهِ نَحْنُ مِن صَالِحِي قَومِنَا، وَبِحَسبِنا أَن

نَكُونَ مِن صَالِحِي قَومِنَا.

222 — Jābir said a group of people came to ʿAlī Ibnil-Husayn, they praised him so he said: "How false and bold are you with Allāh, we are from the best of our people and we seek reward from Allāh for being from the righteous among our people."[4]

---

1 — This is evidence that the Salaf knew that capital punishment for heresy and the likes was the duty of the head of state and not any citizen of a land, regardless of how noble they may be.

2 — Possibly referring to the hadīth of Saʿīd Ibn Zaid who mentioned that the Prophet, Abū Bakr, ʿUmar and ʿUthmān were upon mount Hirā when the mount began to tremor so the Prophet (صَلَّىاللَّهُعَلَيْهِوَسَلَّمَ) said: "Be still Oh Hirā! For indeed upon you is the Prophet, As-Sidīq and the two marytrs." Collected by Abū Dāwūd (3638) and At-Tirmidhī (3757) and declared 'sahīh' by Shaikh Al-Albānī in Sahīh Sunanit-Tirmidhī (3757).

3 — Collected by Abū Nuʿaym in Al-Hilyah (3/185) and Ibn ʿAsākir in Tārīkh Damishq (54/286).

4 — Collected by Ibn Saʿd in At-Tabaqāt (5/214) and Al-Hārith Ibn Abī Usāmah in Al-Musnad (994) and Ibn ʿAsākir in Tārīkh Damishq (41/391).

Benefits from the narration: ʿAlī Ibnil-Husayn Ibn ʿAlī Ibn Abī Tālib, the grandson of ʿAlī ibn Abī Tālib, made it clear to the shiʿah who entered upon him, that the excessive praise that they gave to the household of the Prophet, and the station they had raised the household of the Prophet to, constituted fabricating a lie against Allāh. They raised ʿAlī to the station of the Prophet and some claimed he was Allāh in the flesh, and they went into extremes in raising the station of his offsprings thus ʿAlī Ibnil-Husayn was not affected by the praise they had for him, he declared them liars and then humbly mentioned that the affair was nothing more than the fact that Allāh made them from

[٢٢٣] - وَقَالَ سُلَيْمَانُ بْنُ قَرْمٍ الضَّبِّيُّ: كُنْتُ عِنْدَ عَبْدِ اللَّهِ ابْنِ الحُسَيْنِ بْنِ
الحَسَنِ فَقَالَ لَهُ رَجُلٌ أَصْلَحَكَ اللَّهُ مِنْ أَهْلِ قِبْلَتِنَا أَحَدٌ يَنْبَغِي أَنْ نَشْهَدَ عَلَيْهِ
بِشِرْكٍ؟ قَالَ نَعَمْ الرَّافِضَةُ أَشْهَدُ أَنَّهُمْ لَمُشْرِكُونَ وَكَيْفَ لَا يَكُونُونَ مُشْرِكِينَ وَلَوْ
سَأَلْتَهُمْ أَذْنَبَ النَّبِيُّ صَلَّى اللَّهُ عَلَيْهِ وَسَلَّمَ؟ لَقَالُوا نَعَمْ وَقَدْ غَفَرَ اللَّهُ لَهُ مَا
تَقَدَّمَ مِنْ ذَنْبِهِ وَمَا تَأَخَّرَ وَلَوْ قُلْتَ لَهُمْ أَذْنَبَ عَلِيٌّ؟ لَقَالُوا لَا وَمَنْ قَالَ ذَلِكَ
فَقَدْ كَفَرَ.

223 — Sulaimān Ibn Qarm Adh-Dhabbī[1] said: "I was in the
presence of ʿAbdullāh Ibnil-Husain Ibnil-Hasan and a man said to
him: 'May Allāh rectify you. From the people of our qibla is an
individual against whom we should bear witness that he is upon
shirk!'

He said: 'Yes! The Rāfidhah! I bear witness that they are Mushrikūn!
And how would they not be considered Mushrikūn when if you
were to ask them if the Prophet committed sins he would say *"Yes!"*
— even though Allāh has forgiven his past and future sin! But if you
were to ask them: *"Did ʿAlī sin?"* They would say *"No! And whoever
says he did, has disbelieved!"*'"

•

[٢٢٤] - حَدَّثَنَا أَبُو القَاسِمِ عَبْدُ اللَّهِ بْنُ مُحَمَّدِ بْنِ إِسْحَاقَ المَرْوَزِيُّ قَالَ نَا
عَبَّاسٌ الدُّورِيُّ قَالَ نَا جَعْفَرُ بْنُ عَوْنٍ عَنْ فُضَيْلِ بْنِ مَرْزُوقٍ قَالَ سَمِعْتُ عَبْدَ
اللَّهِ بْنَ حَسَنِ بْنِ حُسَيْنٍ يَقُولُ لِرَجُلٍ مِنَ الرَّافِضَةِ: وَاللَّهِ إِنَّ قَتْلَكَ لَقُرْبَةٌ لَوْلَا
حَقُّ الجِوَارِ.

---

the people of faith and righteousness from their household, and not they they are to be
deified.

1 — He is Sulaimān Ibn Qirm Adh-Dhabbī Al-Kūfī.

224 — Abul-Qāsim 'Abdullāh Ibn Muhammad Ibn Is-hāq Al-Marwazī said it was narrated to me from Abbās Ad-Dūrī who said it was narrated to me from Ja'far Ibn 'Aun Ibn Fudhail Ibn Marzūq who said I heard 'Abdullāh Ibn Hasan Ibn Husain say to a man from the Rāfidhah: "By Allāh! Killing you is a means of drawing near to Allāh, had it not been for the right of the neighbour!"[1]

•

[٢٢٥] - وَقَالَ جَابِرُ بْنُ رِفَاعَةَ سَأَلْتُ جَعْفَرَ بْنَ مُحَمَّدٍ - رضي اللَّه عنه - عَنْ أَبِي بَكْرٍ وَعُمَرَ رَضِيَ اللَّهُ عَنْهُمَا فَقَالَ: لَا أَنَالَنِي اللَّهُ شَفَاعَةَ مُحَمَّدٍ إِنْ لَمْ أَتَقَرَّبْ إِلَى اللَّهِ بِحُبِّهِمَا وَالصَّلَاةِ عَلَيْهِمَا.

225 — Jābir Ibn Rafā'ah[2] said: "I asked Ja'far Ibn Muhammad[3] (رَضِيَ اللَّهُ عَنْهُ) about Abū Bakr and 'Umar (رَضِيَ اللَّهُ عَنْهُمَا) and he said: 'Indeed the intercession of Muhammad will not reach me if I do not draw close to Allāh by loving the two of them, and sending prayers upon the two of them!'"[4]

•

[٢٢٦] - وَقَالَ الْحَسَنُ بْنُ صَالِحٍ: سَأَلْتُ جَعْفَرَ بْنَ مُحَمَّدٍ عَنْ أَبِي بَكْرٍ وَعُمَرَ فَقَالَ: أَبْرَأُ مِنْ كُلِّ مَنْ ذَكَرَهُمَا إِلَّا بِخَيْرٍ قُلْتُ لَعَلَّكَ تَقُولُ ذَاكَ تَقِيَّةً فَقَالَ أَنَا إِذًا مِنَ الْمُشْرِكِينَ وَلَا نَالَتْنِي شَفَاعَةُ مُحَمَّدٍ - (صَلَّى اللَّهُ عَلَيْهِ وَسَلَّمَ) - إِنْ لَمْ أَتَقَرَّبْ إِلَى اللَّهِ - عز وجل - بِحُبِّهِمَا وَلَكِنَّ قَوْمًا يَتَأَكَّلُونَ بِنَا النَّاسُ.

---

1 — *Tārīkh Ibn Ma'īn* (1162) Al-Lillakā'ī: 2804 and 2803.

2 — He is Jābir Ibn Yazīd Ibn Rifā'ah Al-'Ijlī.

3 — He is Ja'far Ibn Muhammad Ibn 'Alī Ibn Husain Ibn 'Alī Ibn Abī Tālib, the great great grandson of 'Alī Ibn Abī Tālib (رَضِيَ اللَّهُ عَنْهُ).

4 — Collected by Ahmad in *Fadhā'ilus-Sahābah* (176) and Al-Lillakā'ī (2465 and 2466) and Al-Baihaqī in *Al-I'tiqād* (p.358).

226 — Al-Hasan Ibn Sālih said: "I asked Ja'far Ibn Muhammad (148H) about Abū Bakr and 'Umar so he said: 'I free myself from anyone who mentions about them except good!'

So I said: 'Perhaps you are saying that using 'taqiyyah'?'[1] He replied: 'May I be from the people of polytheism, and may the intercession of Muhammad (ﷺ) not reach me, if I do not hold that one draws close to Allāh by loving the two of them, but we are those who have been capitalized upon by people.'"[2/3]

•

[٢٢٧] - وَقَالَ أَبُو خَالِدٍ اَلْأَحْمَرَ: سَأَلْتُ عَبْدَ اَللَّهِ بْنَ حَسَنِ بْنِ الْحُسَيْنِ رَضِيَ اللَّهُ عَنْهُمَا عَنْ أَبِي بَكْرٍ وَعُمَرَ رَضِيَ اللَّهُ عَنْهُمَا فَقَالَ صَلَّى اللَّهُ عَلَيْهِمَا وَلَا صَلَّى عَلَى مَنْ لَا يُصَلِّي عَلَيْهِمَا وَنَحْنُ غَدًا بُرَآءُ مِمَّنْ جَعَلْنَا طُعْمَتَهُ.

227 — Abū Khālid Al-Ahmar said: "I asked 'Abdullāh Ibn Hasan Ibn Husain[4] (d. 145H) (رضي الله عنه) about Abū Bakr and 'Umar (رضي الله عنهما) and he said: 'May prayers be upon the two of them, and may no prayers be upon the one who doesn't send prayers upon them, and tomorrow (i.e. in the future) we are free of anyone who takes us for food!'" (i.e. capitalizes upon us.)[5]

•

---

1 — 'Taqiyyah' is the concept believed in by the Rāfidhah of lying for a religious goal.

2 — i.e. People use our names, attribute statements to us, and benefit from that.

3 — Collected by Ad-Dāraqutnī in Fadhā'ilus-Sahābah (69).

4 — He is 'Abdullāh Ibn Hasan Ibn Hasan Ibn 'Alī Ibn Abī Tālib — 'Hasan Ibn Husain' in the text is an error).

5 — Collected by Ad-Dāraqutnī in Fadhā'ilus-Sahābah (55 and 57) and Al-Lillakā'ī (2470).

[٢٢٨] - قَالَ مُحَمَّدُ بْنُ عَلِيِّ بْنِ الحُسَيْنِ: مَنْ فَضَّلْنَا عَلَى أَبِي بَكْرٍ وَعُمَرَ

فَقَدْ بَرِئَ مِنْ سُنَّةِ جَدِّنَا - (صَلَّى ٱللَّهُ عَلَيْهِ وَسَلَّمَ) - وَنَحْنُ خُصَمَاؤُهُ غَدًا عِنْدَ اَللَّهِ - عز

وجل.

228 — Muhammad Ibn 'Alī Ibnil-Husain[1] (114H or 117H) said:
"Whoever gives preference to us over Abū Bakr and 'Umar, then he
is free of the Sunnah of our grandfather[2] (صَلَّى ٱللَّهُ عَلَيْهِ وَسَلَّمَ) and we will be
his opponents tomorrow in front of Allāh."

•

[٢٢٩] - وَقَالَ عَلِيُّ بْنُ أَبِي طَالِبٍ - رضي اللَّه عنه - قَالَ لِيَ النَّبِيُّ -

(صَلَّى ٱللَّهُ عَلَيْهِ وَسَلَّمَ) - «سَيَأْتِي قَوْمٌ لَهُمْ نَبَزٌ يُقَالُ لَهُمْ اَلرَّافِضَةُ أَيْنَ لَقِيتُهُمْ فَاقْتُلُوهُمْ

فَإِنَّهُمْ مُشْرِكُونَ.» قُلْتُ: يَا رَسُولَ اَللَّهِ وَمَا اَلْعَلَامَةُ فِيهِمْ؟ قَالَ: «يُقَرِّظُونَكَ بِمَا

لَيْسَ فِيكَ وَيَطْعَنُونَ عَلَى السَّلَفِ.»

229 — 'Alī Ibn Abī Tālib said: "The Prophet (صَلَّى ٱللَّهُ عَلَيْهِ وَسَلَّمَ) said to
me: 'There will come a people who shall be named the Rāfidhah
wherever you find them kill them for indeed they are Mushrikūn.'
So I said: 'Oh Messenger of Allāh! What is their sign?' He said:
'They will praise you (an address to 'Alī himself) with that which
you do not possess (i.e. overpraise you) and they will speak ill of the
(pious) predecessors.'"[3]

---

1 — He is Muhammad Ibn 'Alī Ibnil-Husain Ibn 'Alī Ibn Abī Tālib, Abū Ja'far Al-
Bāqir.

2 — Referring here to the Prophet (صَلَّى ٱللَّهُ عَلَيْهِ وَسَلَّمَ). He was actually his great-great-great-
grandfather. The term 'grandfather' may be used in a general way in the Arabic language
to refer to forefather.

3 — Collected by Ibn Abī 'Āsim in As-Sunnah (1013 and 1014) and At-Tabarānī in Al-
Awsat (6605) and Al-Ājjurī in Ash-Shari'ah (2008) and declared 'da'īf' (weak) by Shaikh
Al-Albānī in Dhilālul-Jannah (979) and he declares the slightly longer version 'da'īf jiddan'
(very weak) (980).

[٢٣٠] - وَقَالَ عَلِيٌّ (رَضِيَ اللَّهُ عَنْهُ) تَفْتَرِقُ هَذِهِ الْأُمَّةُ عَلَى نَيِّفٍ وَسَبْعِينَ فِرْقَةً شَرُّهَا فِرْقَةٌ تَنْتَحِلُ حُبَّنَا وَتُخَالِفُ أَمْرَنَا.

230 — ʿAlī (رَضِيَ اللَّهُ عَنْهُ) said: "This Ummah will split into seventy-odd sects. The worst of them will be a group who claim religious love for us (referring to the household of the Prophet (صَلَّى اللَّهُ عَلَيْهِ وَسَلَّمَ)) but will oppose our affair."[1]

•

[٢٣١] - وَقَالَ عَلِيٌّ (رَضِيَ اللَّهُ عَنْهُ) يَهْلِكُ فِيَّ رَجُلَانِ مُحِبٌّ مُفْرِطٌ وَمُبْغِضٌ مُفْتَرٍ.

231 — ʿAlī (رَضِيَ اللَّهُ عَنْهُ) said: "Two types of individuals will be destroyed due to (their stance regarding) me. The one who loves me excessively and the one who hates me and fabricates lies against me."[2]

•

[٢٣٢] - قَالَ حَدَّثَنَا أَبُو بَكْرٍ عَبْدُ اللَّهِ بْنُ مُحَمَّدِ بْنِ زِيَادٍ النَّيْسَابُورِيُّ قَالَ نَا عَبْدُ الْمَلِكِ بْنُ عَبْدِ الْحَمِيدِ الْمَيْمُونِيُّ: قَالَ لِي أَحْمَدُ ابْنُ حَنْبَلٍ رَحْمَةُ اللَّهِ عَلَيْهِ يَا أَبَا الْحَسَنِ إِذَا رَأَيْتَ رَجُلاً يَذْكُرُ رَجُلاً مِنْ أَصْحَابِ رَسُولِ اللَّهِ (صَلَّى اللَّهُ عَلَيْهِ وَسَلَّمَ) بِسُوءٍ فَاتَّهِمْهُ عَلَى الْإِسْلَامِ.

232 — Abū Bakr ʿAbdullāh Ibn Muhammad Ibn Ziyād An-Naisābūrī narrated to me and said: "It was narrated to me from ʿAbdul-Mālik Ibn ʿAbdul-Hamīd Al-Maimūnī who said Ahmad Ibn Hanbal (رَحِمَهُ اللَّهُ) said to me: 'Oh Abul-Hasan. If you see a man

1 — Collected by Abū Nuʿaym in *Al-Hilyah* (5/8).

2 — Collected by Ibn Abī Shaibah in *Al-Musannaf* (32134 and 32136) and Ahmad in *Al-Musnad* (1/160) and in *Fadhāʾilus-Sahābah* (951) Al-Lillakāʾī (268).

speaking ill of one of the companions of the Messenger of Allāh, then suspect his Islām!'"[1]

•

[٢٣٣] - وَقَالَ عَلِيُّ بْنِ أَبِي طَالِبٍ: قَالَ لِي النَّبِيُّ - (صَلَّىٱللَّهُعَلَيْهِوَسَلَّمَ) - يَخْرُجُ قَبْلَ

قِيَامِ السَّاعَةِ قَوْمٌ يُقَالُ لَهُمْ الرَّافِضَةُ بُرَآءُ مِنْ الإسْلام.

233 — 'Alī Ibn Abī Tālib said: "The Prophet (صَلَّىٱللَّهُعَلَيْهِوَسَلَّمَ) said to me: 'Before the establishment of the hour there will come a people who will be referred to as the Rāfidhah, they are free from Islām!'"[2]

•

[٢٣٣] - قَالَ حَدَّثَنَا القَاضِي ابْنُ مُطَرِّفٍ قَالَ حَدَّثَنَا مُحَمَّدُ بْنُ أَحْمَدَ بْنِ

مُحَمَّدٍ قَالَ لَنَا مُحَمَّدُ بْنُ أَحْمَدَ بْنِ خَالِدٍ قَالَ حَدَّثَنَا أَبُو عَبْدِ اللَّهِ الْمُؤَدِّبُ

الْمَعْرُوفِ بِابْنِ شَاخِيلٍ قَالَ حَدَّثَنِي يَزِيدُ بْنُ مُحَمَّدٍ الثَّقَفِيٌّ قَالَ نَا حنان بْن

سَدِير عَن سَدِير، عن محمد بن علي، عَن آبَائِهِ، قَالَ: قَالَ عليٌّ لِنَوْفٍ

الْبِكَالِيِّ وَهُوَ مَعَهُ السَّطْحُ - يَا نَوْفُ - تَدْرِي مَنْ شِيعَتِي؟ قَالَ لَا وَاللَّهِ قَالَ

شِيعَتِي الذِّيلُ الشِّفَاهِ الْخُمْصُ الْبُطُونِ تَعْرِفُ الرَّهْبَانِيَّةَ وَالرَّبَّانِيَّةَ فِي وُجُوهِهِمْ

رُهْبَانٌ بِاللَّيْلِ أَسْدٌ بِالنَّهَارِ إِذَا جَنَّهُمْ اللَّيْلُ اتّْزَرُوا عَلَى أَوْسَاطِهِمْ وَارْتَدُّوا عَلَى

أَطْرَافِهِمْ يَخُرُّونَ كَمَا تَخُورُ الثِّيرَانُ فِي فِكَاكِ رِقَابِهِمْ، شِيعَتِي الَّذِينَ إِذَا شَهِدُوا

لَمْ يُعْرَفُوا وَإِذَا خَطَبُوا لَمْ يُزَوَّجُوا وَإِذَا مَرِضُوا لَمْ يُعَادُوا وَإِذَا غَابُوا لَمْ يُفْتَقَدُوا

شِيعَتِي الَّذِينَ فِي أَمْوَالِهِمْ يَتَوَاسَوْنَ وَفِي اللَّهِ يَتَبَاذَلُونَ دِرْهَمْ وَفَلْسٍ وَثَوْبٍ

وَثَوْبٍ وَإِلَّا فَلَا شِيعَتِي مَنْ لَمْ يَهِرُّ هَرِيرَ الكِلَابِ وَلَمْ يَطْمَعْ طَمَعَ الغُرَابِ لَا

1 — Collected by Al-Lillakā'ī (2359) and Ibn 'Asākir in *Tārīkh Dimashq* (59/209).

2 — Collected by 'Abdullāh Ibn Ahmad in *As-Sunnah* (1271) and Al-Baihaqī in *Dalā'ilun-Nubuwwah* (6/547).

يَسْأَلُ النَّاسَ وَإِنْ مَاتَ جُوعًا، إِنْ رَأَى مُؤْمِنًا أَكْرَمَهُ وَإِنْ رَأَى فَاسِقًا هَجَرَهُ،

هَؤُلَاءِ وَاللَّهِ يَانَوْفُ شِيعَتِي شُرُورُهُمْ مَأْمُونَةٌ وَقُلُوبُهُمْ مَحْزُونَةٌ وَحَوَائِجُهُمْ خَفِيفَةٌ

وَأَنْفُسُهُمْ عَفِيفَةٌ إِنْ اِخْتَلَفَتْ بِهِمُ الْبُلْدَانُ لَمْ تَخْتَلِفْ قُلُوبُهُمْ أَمَّا اللَّيْلُ فَصَافُّونَ

أَقْدَامَهُمْ يَفْتَرِشُونَ جِبَاهَهُمْ تَجْرِي دُمُوعُهُمْ عَلَى خُدُودِهِمْ يَجْأَرُونَ فِي فِكَاكِ

رِقَابِهِمْ وَأَمَّا النَّهَارُ فَحُلَمَاءُ عُلَمَاءُ نُجَبَاءُ كِرَامٌ أَبْرَارٌ أَتْقِيَاءُ، يَا نَوْفُ شِيعَتِي

أَلَّذِينَ اِتَّخَذُوا الْأَرْضَ بِسَاطًا وَالْمَاءِ طِيبًا وَالْقُرْآنَ شِعَارًا وَالدُّعَاءَ دِثَارًا قَرَضُوا

الدُّنْيَا قَرْضًا عَلَى دِينٍ مِنْهَاجِ عِيسَى اِبْنِ مَرْيَمَ عَلَيْهِ اَلسَّلَامُ.

234 — The Judge, Ibn Mutarrif narrated to us and said: Muhammad Ibn Ahmad Ibn Muhammad narrated to me and said: Muhammad Ibn Ahmad Ibn Khālid narrated to me and said: Abū ʿAbdillāh Al-Muʾaddib who was known as Ibn Shākhīl said: Yazīd Ibn Muhammad Ath-Thaqafī narrated to me and said: Hasan Ibn Sadīr who said: Upon the authority of Sadīr who narrated upon the authority of Muhammad Ibn ʿAlī from his father who said: ʿAlī (رَضِيَاللَّهُعَنْهُ) said to Nauf Al-Bikāli[1] (after 90H) when he was with him upon a rooftop: "Oh Nauf, do you know who my Shīʿah (group/party) is?"

He said: "No by Allāh!"

He said: "My Shīʿah, are those who have dry lips and empty bellies, those whose rahbāniyah (their worship of their lord) and rabbāniyah (their veneration of their lord) may be seen in their faces. Ruhbān (staunch worshippers) by night, lions by day. When night falls, they wrap their lower bodies and cover their upper limbs, they cry out (to their lord) the way a bull bellows, seeking (from their lord) to free their necks (from the fire).

My Shīʿah, are those who, if they were to give testimony they would not be known, and if they made a proposal for marriage their

1 — He is Nauf Ibn Fadhālah Al-Bikālī.

offers would not be accepted. If they are sick they are not visited, and if they are absent they are not inquired about.

My Shī'ah, are those who advise each other concerning (the correct) use of wealth, those who sacrifice and spend their wealth in the way of Allāh. (Giving) *dirhams* then another, and *fils*[1] then another, and garments then another, and if they do not have, they do not give. My Shī'ah are not those who growl with the growling of dogs, nor pursue (worldly affairs) with the covetousness of crows, neither do they ask of the people even if they were to die of hunger. If they see a believer, they deal with him honourably, and if they see a *fāsiq* (evildoer) they boycott him.

These by Allāh, Oh Nauf, are my Shī'ah. One is safe from any evil coming from them, their hearts grieve, and their needs are small. They are chaste, and even if they live in different lands, their hearts do not differ.

As for by night, then they arrange their feet (for prayer), and their carpets clothe their foreheads (meaning they fall prostrate upon the carpet), their tears run down their cheeks, seeking for their necks to be freed (from Allāh's punishment). As for by day, then they are forbearing people of knowledge, generous and bountiful, righteous and god-fearing. Oh Nauf, indeed my Shī'ah are those who have taken the earth as their carpet, and water as their perfume and (reading) the Qur'ān as their motto, and supplication as their robe. They have used the loan of their dunya, to repay the debt of their dīn, (upon) the methodology of 'Īsā Ibn Maryam – (عَلَيْهِ السَّلَام)."[2]

---

1 — *Dirhams* and *Fils* were two types of coins, used as currency in that time.

2 — Collected by Ibn Fākhir in his *Juz'* (p.211) and Ibn 'Asākir in his *Tārīkh Dimashq* (62/305-306) and 'Abdullāh Ibn Ahmad in *Zawā'id Zuhd* (1144). This narration is not established upon 'Alī. In its chain of transmission there are other weak narrators such as Sadīr Ibn Hakīm Ibn Suhaib who was an extreme Rāfidhi and considered a *Kadhāb* (liar) by the scholars of hadīth (Such as Sufyān Ibn 'Uyainah), as was his son Hanān.

Donate to the Cause

ONLINE:

salafibookstore.com/donate

Make a one-time donation, or set up a monthly subscription. It takes less than a minute!

VIA BANK TRANSFER:

Account Name — Salafi Bookstore & Islamic Centre
Bank — Lloyds Bank Plc.
Branch — Erdington, Birmingham, UK.
Account Number — 002 312 60
Sort Code — 30-93-09
BIC/Swift Code — LOYDGB21282.

IBAN — GB14 LOYD 3093 0900 2312 60

Specify a reference such as: "books," "leaflets," "masjid", etc. Please also consider making this a recurring donation. Note: the IBAN and BIC codes are for foreign accounts.

Visit Our Websites

SALAFISOUNDS.COM — *For authentic Islamic audio.*

SALAF.COM — *Your starting point for Islām, Sunnah, & Salafiyyah online.*

AQIDAH.COM — *Learn the creed of Ahlus-Sunnah wal-Jamāʿah.*

SALAFIMASJID.COM — *The online home of the Salafi Masjid, on Wright St.*

AH-SP.COM — *The website of the author of this book; Abū Hakeem Bilāl Davis.*

ABUKHADEEJAH.COM — *The website of Abū Khadeejah ʿAbdul-Wāhid.*

SALAFIBOOKSTORE.COM — *Your one-stop-shop for Islamic literature and effects.*

SALAFIPUBS.COM — *Salafi Digital Media.*